Exploration in the World of the Ancients

Revised Edition

DISCOVERY & EXPLORATION

Exploration in the World of the Ancients,
  Revised Edition

Exploration in the World of the Middle Ages,
  500–1500, Revised Edition

Exploration in the Age of Empire, 1750–1953,
  Revised Edition

Exploring the Pacific, Revised Edition

Exploring the Polar Regions, Revised Edition

Discovery of the Americas, 1492–1800,
  Revised Edition

Opening Up North America, 1497–1800,
  Revised Edition

Across America: The Lewis and Clark Expedition,
  Revised Edition

Exploring North America, 1800–1900, Revised Edition

Exploring Space, Revised Edition

DISCOVERY & EXPLORATION

Exploration in the World of the Ancients

Revised Edition

JOHN S. BOWMAN

JOHN S. BOWMAN and MAURICE ISSERMAN
General Editors

CHELSEA HOUSE
PUBLISHERS
An imprint of Infobase Publishing

Exploration in the World of the Ancients, Revised Edition

Copyright ©2010 by Infobase Publishing

All rights reserved. No part of this book may be reproduced or utilized in any form or by any means, electronic or mechanical, including photocopying, recording, or by any information storage or retrieval systems, without permission in writing from the publisher. For information contact:

Chelsea House
An imprint of Infobase Publishing
132 West 31st Street
New York, NY 10001

Library of Congress Cataloging-in-Publication Data
Bowman, John Stewart, 1931–
  Exploration in the world of the ancients / by John S. Bowman ; John S. Bowman and Maurice Isserman, General Editors. — Rev. ed.
      p. cm. — (Discovery and exploration)
  Includes bibliographical references and index.
  ISBN 978-1-60413-191-8 (hardcover)
  1. Geography, Ancient—Juvenile literature. 2. Discoveries in geography—Juvenile literature. I. Isserman, Maurice. II. Title. III. Series.
  G86.B68 2010
  913--dc22
                                    2009018849

Chelsea House books are available at special discounts when purchased in bulk quantities for businesses, associations, institutions, or sales promotions. Please call our Special Sales Department in New York at (212) 967-8800 or (800) 322-8755.

You can find Chelsea House on the World Wide Web at
http://www.chelseahouse.com

Text design by Erika K. Arroyo
Cover design by Keith Trego

Printed in the United States of America

Bang EJB 10 9 8 7 6 5 4 3 2 1

This book is printed on acid-free paper.

All links and Web addresses were checked and verified to be correct at the time of publication. Because of the dynamic nature of the Web, some addresses and links may have changed since publication and may no longer be valid.

Contents

1

Pytheas Explores the North

ABOUT 315 B.C., PYTHEAS, A CITIZEN OF THE GREEK COLONY OF Massalia, headed his ship west to the Pillars of Hercules. This was the ancient Greeks' name for the Strait of Gibraltar, the body of water between Gibraltar and North Africa. (A Greek myth tells that Hercules had placed two rocks to guard the strait.) To pass through this strait at that period of history was a major undertaking. Beyond the strait were the unknown waters and lands of the North Atlantic region. Pytheas had set his sights on just such a voyage.

A DANGEROUS TRIP

Even before he reached the Pillars of Hercules, Pytheas faced potential dangers. Massalia had been founded about 600 B.C. by Greeks from the city of Phocea on the coast of Asia Minor (modern Foca, in Turkey). In the centuries since, it had grown and prospered as a center of Greek culture and commerce in the western Mediterranean. Located just east of the mouth of the Rhone River, Massalia served as an *entrepôt*, or trading center, for merchants from all over the Mediterranean and merchants who came down the Rhone from northwestern Europe.

During those same centuries, another city on the opposite shore of the Mediterranean had also grown powerful and prosperous. This was Carthage, on the coast of North Africa (modern Tunisia) almost due south of Massalia. The Carthaginians were an assertive people who wanted to control trade in the western Mediterranean. They had built their own colonies along the coast of Spain, and they did not take kindly

The Rock of Gibraltar, just off the south coast of Spain, was considered by the ancient Greeks as one of the Pillars of Hercules. Beyond this pillar of Hercules and the other pillar, Jebel Musa, on the African side of the strait, lay an ocean largely unknown to ancient Mediterranean sailors.

to the Greeks who also wanted a share of the commerce. Their colony of Gades (present-day Cadiz) was on the coast of Spain just outside the Pillars of Hercules. Gades could cut off Greeks or others who might seek to sail out of the Mediterranean.

Pytheas sailed from Massalia along the south coast of France, down the east coast of Spain, and through the Pillars of Hercules. He then continued along the southern coast of Spain and Portugal. He must have been very clever or lucky to avoid any conflict with Carthaginians while passing Gades. Ships in that era sailed and rowed quite close to the coast during the day.

Pytheas's ship, by the way, was most likely a merchant, or cargo, ship. It was not a warship. Those were the two major types of ships at this time. Warships were designed for speed and strength. They were relatively shallow, long, and trim. Many oarsmen propelled them. This type of ship was not practical for a long voyage. Merchant ships were designed to hold cargo and so were deeper, broader, and sturdy. Most merchant ships were propelled by one large sail attached to a central mast. Some merchant ships also had several oarsmen rowing on each side. Both warships and merchant ships were steered mainly by large oars at the stern, or the rear, of the ships.

Pytheas's ship probably had oarsmen—perhaps 10 on each side. His total crew may have been about 30 men. The oarsmen helped the ship to make some progress when there was no favorable wind. Even so, the ship probably only averaged about five or six miles an hour. On a long day they might cover some 50 miles (80 kilometers). The energy expended on keeping such a ship moving must have required a fair amount of calories and liquids for the crew, so they had to pull their ship ashore each night to replenish their food and water supplies.

THE JOURNEY

Once past the southwestern corner of the Iberian Peninsula, Pytheas sailed northward along the Atlantic coast of Portugal and northwestern Spain. Continuing north, he almost certainly stayed fairly close to the coast until he arrived at the great peninsula of Brittany. Eventually, he arrived at the island of Ushant, the westernmost point of present-day France. There he had to make one of his longest "runs" in the open sea, sailing 100 miles (160.9 km) to reach the southwestern coast of England. The trip took about 24 hours. Once there he reached the region known to him as Belerion, today known as Land's End. It lies in Cornwall, England's southwesternmost region.

Pytheas may not have been the first Mediterranean mariner to have sailed this route, although he would be the first to provide a written report of many of the features of the coast. (The book he wrote has never been found, but during the following centuries many ancient writers quoted from it.) When Pytheas reached England, his voyage becomes a major contribution to the history of exploration. The people of the Mediterranean knew little about the British Isles. What they did know, though, is that a particular material came from somewhere in that region: tin.

Tin was among the scarcest and the most valued products sought by the peoples of the Mediterranean. For 3,000 years, they had been mixing tin with copper to form a harder material, bronze. Bronze was used for making everything from weapons to religious objects, from armor to jewelry, from tools to coins, from statues to drinking vessels. Copper was relatively plentiful around the Mediterranean. Tin, however, was rare. For centuries, tin had been imported into the Mediterranean region

ANCIENT NAVIGATION

In the thousands of years before Pytheas, and for at least another 1,500 years, the knowledge, skills, and tools used for navigating ships hardly changed. Most sailors basically depended on *dead reckoning*. They estimated their location at sea based on distance traveled and the time elapsed, modified by such matters as position of the sun and the strength of the winds. Furthermore, they depended on common knowledge, such as familiar landmarks, the rising and setting of the sun, and the positions of certain stars and planets.

Knowing familiar landmarks such as rivers, cliffs, towns, and buildings was not enough. Navigators had to know about the possible dangers near shore. These included reefs, rocks, and treacherous currents. All such knowledge was learned by experience and then passed on by word of mouth.

Probably the only tool that these early sailors used was a sounding rod, or line. This tool was simply rope with a lead weight attached to one end. It measured the depth of the water at any given point. The navigator dropped the line overboard until it hit bottom. The more sophisticated lead weights had a little hollow at the bottom that was filled with tallow or grease. When it was brought to the surface, it revealed the nature of the ocean floor. Experienced sailors could tell a lot from this.

In the Greek language, the helmsman of a ship who also served as the navigator was known as a *kybernetes*—"governor." This became the root of the modern word *cybernetics*—the science of control and communications processes, and this in turn has provided the prefix, *cyber-* for any number of words involving "navigation" by computers. So it is that today's most advanced technology links itself to the basic but intelligent skills of ancient navigation.

from northwestern Spain and the British Isles. After being extracted from its rocky ore, the metal was transported overland through Spain or France to the shores of the Mediterranean.

Massalia was one of the major trading centers for tin. However, most of the Mediterraneans involved in this trade depended on the middlemen who moved the tin overland from its source. This added a lot to the price. There were rumors of rich tin mines on islands in that northern ocean. Indeed, the Greeks' word for "tin," *kassiteros,* had been given to the distant islands believed to be the source of tin, the Cassiterides. Evidently some of the merchants of Massalia wanted to make direct contact with those miners, and that seems to have been one of the chief goals of Pytheas's expedition—to find those tin mines. When Pytheas arrived at the islands off Cornwall, he was convinced he had found that place.

In fact, he soon discovered that the tin mines were on the mainland of Cornwall. Pytheas described the miners' work:

They extract the tin from its bed by a cunning process. The bed is of rock, but contains earthy interstices, along which they cut a gallery. Having melted the tin and refined it, they hammer it into knucklebone shape and convey it to an adjacent island named Ictis [possibly St. Michael's Mount off the coast of Cornwall].

Pytheas believed that he had found the source of the tin and most likely loaded his boat with some. He then sailed completely around Great Britain. He measured the coastline by estimating the length of land passed each day. Pytheas's measurements were surprisingly exact: "Britain is triangular like Sicily, with three unequal sides." Pytheas did more than sail along the coast although most scholars cannot believe his claim that "I traversed the whole of Britannike accessible by foot." He does seem to have made occasional visits into the interior and reported on the people he met:

The inhabitants of Britain are said to have sprung from the soil and to preserve a primitive style of life. They make use of chariots in war, such as the ancient Greek heroes are reputed to have employed in the Trojan War; and their habitations are rough-and-ready, being for the most part constructed of wattles or logs. . . . They are simple in their habits and far removed from the cunning and knavishness of modern man.

He eventually reached the northern coast of Scotland. There, Pytheas was told about the island of Thule, which he claimed was six days' sail north of Britain. He did not venture that far. He did, however, report that around Thule "there is neither sea nor air but a mixture like sea-lung, in which earth and air are suspended." Exactly what he meant by "sea-lung" would never be known for sure. Some say he was describing jellyfish, some say slushy ice. It is very likely that he was describing the thick, clammy fogs of the North Atlantic. He also described large fish blowing out sprays of water—obviously whales. As for Thule itself, some claim it is Iceland, others Norway, still others the Shetland Islands. In any case, Pytheas also reported that Thule was so far north that, in the middle of summer, the sun went down for only two or three hours. In general, much of what Pytheas would describe and report was a mixture of the truth and misunderstanding.

After completing his journey around Great Britain, Pytheas returned across the Channel to the coast of France or Belgium. He then sailed north along the coasts of the Netherlands and Germany. Exactly how far he sailed is not known. It does appear he moved into the North Sea. He may have sailed as far as the mouth of the Elbe River, where he probably turned back when he confronted the great peninsula topped by Denmark.

On his trip home, Pytheas stuck close to the coast of western Europe. He appears to have arrived safely home in Massalia. His journey covered 7,500 miles (12,070 km), longer than Christopher Columbus's trips to the New World. Unlike Columbus's voyage, what happened as a result of Pytheas's voyage is unknown. Nothing seems to have changed in the tin trade, for instance. As for Pytheas, he vanishes from history. Even the book or report he wrote about his voyage did not survive in its original copy.

(opposite page) Greek geographer and explorer Pytheas sailed from Massalia (modern Marseilles, France) to unknown lands of the North Atlantic. He hoped to find the tin mines on the islands in that ocean.

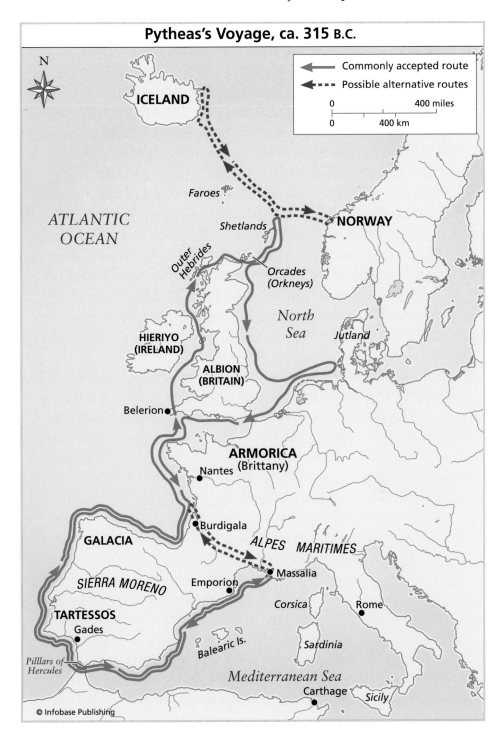

Pytheas's Voyage, ca. 315 B.C.

N

Commonly accepted route
Possible alternative routes

0   400 miles
0   400 km

ICELAND

Faroes

ATLANTIC
OCEAN

Shetlands

NORWAY

Outer
Hebrides

Orcades
(Orkneys)

North
Sea

Jutland

HIERIYO
(IRELAND)

ALBION
(BRITAIN)

Belerion

ARMORICA
(Brittany)

Nantes

Burdigala

GALACIA

ALPES   MARITIMES

Massalia

SIERRA MORENO

Emporion

Corsica

Rome

TARTESSOS

Gades

Balearic Is.

Sardinia

Pillars of
Hercules

Mediterranean Sea

Carthage   Sicily

© Infobase Publishing

THE SIGNIFICANCE OF PYTHEAS

Nothing is known about Pytheas before or after his voyage. He is known only from the writings of several ancient Greeks and Romans. Ironically, several of the writers who describe Pytheas regarded him as a liar. They did not believe he had made the voyage or discovered the things he described. Although some of these ancient writers quote long passages from the report written by Pytheas—it is these secondhand quotations that have been cited here—no part of the original has survived.

If so little is known of the man, why is Pytheas important? Some of the ancient texts suggest that Pytheas was a poor man. He was of no great distinction, but simply undertook the voyage as a commercial venture. He must have had the backing of wealthier merchants in Massalia who wanted him to find the tin mines. This discovery would let the merchants buy tin directly and outmaneuver the Carthaginians in their attempt to monopolize the tin trade. Not only that, the Massalians might then cut out the middlemen involved in the overland route down across France.

Pytheas must have been at least partially motivated by the prospects of profit. If not a prosperous merchant himself, he must have appreciated what lay in store for him should he complete such a voyage. At the same time, it is highly unlikely that a poor man could ever have been able to finance the ship and crew necessary for such an expedition. So if he was relatively poor, he must have had enough of a reputation that the merchants of Massalia supported him.

Whoever he was, whatever caused him to take such a voyage, Pytheas must have been a master sailor. Sailing a ship for thousands of miles in those days was no easy feat. Most ships never sailed that far from their home ports. Although the Mediterranean Sea extended some 2,200 miles (3,540 km) from the eastern shores to the Pillars of Hercules and 600 miles (956 km) at its widest, most mariners at this time would never have considered trying to sail such distances. They never ventured far from coasts and sailed only in familiar waters. They knew the winds, they knew the stars, and they knew the dangers lurking beneath the waves. However, Pytheas sailed into completely unknown, uncharted seas. There were no maps or charts, no familiar landmarks, and no way to know about the reefs or rocks as he approached a shore. He had to be a master mariner, a master navigator.

Some of those who wrote about Pytheas treated him as a serious astronomer. They credited him with believing—rightfully—that there was no star precisely over the North Pole. At least one ancient text said that he set off on his trip to confirm this claim. He was one of the first to be credited with connecting the moon to the rise and fall of the tides. Also, by carefully calculating the changing position of the sun and the length of shadows, he was able to calculate the latitude of Massalia. On his voyage, he recorded the lengthening of the days as they proceeded northward. By observing the height of the sun, he calculated the latitude at various points along the way. Many geographers and mapmakers who followed Pytheas used his latitude for Massalia as the basis for calculating the latitudes of other points in the known world.

There was another skill that Pytheas must have had to complete his voyage. It was not enough to guide a ship safely through hundreds of miles of ocean. The ship had a crew, most likely about 30, including oarsmen, sail crew, and officers. These men needed food and drink, day after day. They put into shore every night and probably often stayed several days to replenish their food supplies—sending out hunting parties and water seekers. Men probably got sick or injured. His ship must have occasionally required repairs. Often he had to deal with the native inhabitants. He probably carried some cargo that he could use as barter, that is, to trade for vital supplies. So Pytheas had to be a good leader of men. He had to be someone who could inspire his crew to keep going, against all odds.

In recent times, some speak of Pytheas as though he was a lone adventurer. They believe he set out to explore for the sake of learning about the unknown. That is probably too modern a notion of such a man and such a trip. However, there had to be something of the adventurer in Pytheas. No one could have forced him to undertake such a voyage. Meanwhile, there must have been hundreds, even thousands of sailors in Massalia who did *not* choose to go. Pytheas had to have some special spark, some special vision. He certainly had to have courage. He had the willingness to set forth into the unknown. He had to have the guts to face all that nature and humans might throw at him. Pytheas had physical strength, too. He must have faced hardships of many kinds: storms at sea, food shortages, and accidents and injuries.

It turns out, then, that Pytheas must have combined in himself many of the main elements that will be found in explorers across the ages and of all cultures. Not all explorers had all these qualities and character-istics and skills, but they had to have some of them. Some would be driven primarily by the chance to become wealthy, often expressed as a desire to seek gold. Even if they had that personal goal, however, many, like Pytheas, needed to gain the support of others.

Like Pytheas, almost all explorers had to have the knowledge and skills either to navigate ships or conduct expeditions across unknown terrain. They had to be able to organize an expedition—provide the food and shelter needed, and maintain the ships or the animals. They had to be able to hold the members of their expeditions together through thick and thin. Some explorers, it is true, were motivated by an almost pure desire for understanding the world—advancing the sciences, adding to knowledge, enlarging the known. But all must have had some sense of adventure. Even the most scientific of explorers had to have the courage to leave the library or the laboratory and confront unknown challenges. Possibly, too, they had a touch of ego to think that they could carry off what lesser men could not.

Finally, what links Pytheas to many of the great explorers who fol-lowed, but distinguishes him from most who went before him, is that he wrote an account of his voyage. He was wrong about many of the details he described. Many people in his own time did not believe him. However, he brought these distant lands into the light of human aware-ness. It was not enough to travel bravely to distant lands. Unless some record was made, some report, even contemporaries would not know for certain what lay out there, and posterity would definitely not know. There have been explorers who have personally shown little or no inter-est in recording their discoveries. However, one way or another, some-one must set down an account for the world to profit. It is the report of the voyage that adds to our steadily growing realm of the known.

Most explorers before Pytheas did not record their adventures. This does not mean that the world had not been explored. Clearly there were people living all over the earth by the time Pytheas made his voyage of "discovery." Before giving credit to the many brave explorers known to have followed Pytheas, it seems necessary to recognize the many anon-ymous people who were truly the first to open up the world.

2

The Original Explorers

PYTHEAS, THE ANCIENT GREEK SAILOR, WAS BY NO MEANS THE FIRST person to travel in the lands and seas he explored. He owes his fame to the fact that he wrote about his voyage. There is another lesson to be learned from his voyage of "discovery": The lands Pytheas visited and explored were inhabited.

This is true for many if not most of the "discoverers" and explorers. They were not the first people to be present in the lands and waters connected to their names and feats. This is as true of the oldest-known ancient explorers as with the twentieth century's great explorers. Except for expeditions in the polar regions and space, most explorers have been going into regions already inhabited or traveled.

The *ancient world* is often defined as beginning with the first writing. Writing appeared at different times in different regions of the world. It does tend to appear about the same time in many places—about 3500 to 3000 B.C. That is when writing, or at least characters, symbols, or drawings of some kind, appears to be recording information.

Before that time is what is known as *prehistory*. Tools, bones, and other kinds of physical evidence are needed to trace the presence of human beings for this period. At that point, archaeologists and anthropologists usually take over from historians. They are the ones who find out when and where human beings first appeared. It can be argued that it is these first human beings in each part of the world who deserve to be known as the first discoverers and explorers.

THE EARLIEST EXPLORERS

The earliest ancestors of human beings are called hominids. Almost all experts agree that the hominids first appeared in East and southern Africa. The first human ancestors, known as *Homo erectus* ("erect man"), appeared about 1.8 million years ago. Not long after that, these primitive beings began to show up in places far from their original sites, specifically in China, India, and Java. Most experts believe that these hominids made their way up Africa's east coast, across Egypt, and then wandered all the way across Asia. Human fossils found in Europe show that *Homo erectus* lived there as early as one million years ago.

Why did they travel so far and in different directions? The answers can probably never be known. Something caused these hominids to keep moving forward into unknown lands. Perhaps this drive is what distinguishes them both as humans themselves and as ancestors of later humans.

The next major stage of human evolution occurred about 500,000 to 160,000 years ago, when the *Homo sapiens* ("wise man") appeared. *Homo sapiens* showed up first in Africa but within 30,000 years they were also in China, India, the Middle East, central Asia, and Europe. Their physical remains are found across Europe, from England to Greece, in remote parts of Uzbekistan, and throughout eastern China. These people were opening up new lands.

Then, by at least 130,000 years ago, *Homo sapiens sapiens* appeared. All human beings today belong to this group. The oldest known fossils have been found in Africa, but similar fossils almost as old have been found in other places, leading to two competing theories. One of them, sometimes called the "Out of Africa Hypothesis," claims that the new species evolved in Africa and about 55,000 years ago migrated up to the Middle East. Some individuals then split off and went over into India and Southeast Asia and east Asia. Others went up into central Asia and split into groups, one at least going west into Europe, another heading farther east into northeastern Asia. As they moved, this new species displaced any local populations of archaic *Homo sapiens*.

The other theory, sometimes known as "The Regional Continuity Hypothesis," claims that the *Homo sapiens sapiens* in each region evolved from the archaic *Homo sapiens* living in that region. However, even in this theory, all modern humans are fundamentally the same

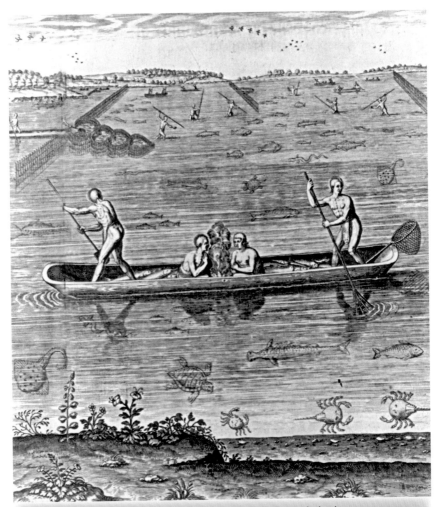

It is assumed that some of the earliest watercraft made by humans were like the crude boats shown in this drawing by John White of the Roanoke Indians. These dugout canoes made from hollowed-out tree trunks were used to travel to islands such as Australia.

because their common ancestors, the archaic *Homo sapiens,* were the same. Whatever the origins, *Homo sapiens sapiens* were clearly on the move. Not only did they spread throughout ever-farther parts of the main landmasses of Europe and Asia, they moved into several new regions. In Southeast Asia, they moved into the lands known today as Burma (Myanmar), Cambodia, Indonesia, Laos, Thailand, and Vietnam. They also moved into faraway islands such as Sri Lanka, the

THE FIRST WATERCRAFT

The oldest known boats to survive were found in Egyptian tombs dated to 2500 B.C. These have survived only because the Egyptians buried them in such dry places that they did not rot away. Long before the Egyptians' sophisticated boats, though, there had to have been all kinds of simple watercraft. It is evident from the evidence of human presence at several locations that at least some early humans did get around on the water.

Undoubtedly, the first watercrafts were simply rafts made of plant materials. Even the most primitive people would have observed that large branches floated. From that, it must have been an easy step to realize that if a large log could float, that log could be hollowed out to hold a person. Rafts and simple dugout canoes must have provided water transportation for thousands of years. Canoes made of bark may also have appeared very early. Because these watercrafts were made of plant material, and because they got wet, they rotted away without leaving a trace behind.

At some point, people in various parts of the world would have begun to devise variations of these two basic craft. Depending on the plants in their region, they would have made rafts of reed, for example. Likewise, canoemakers would have found some trees made lighter and more manageable boats. Meanwhile, some people realized they could sew skins together and stretch them around a light wooden frame to form a type of boat called a coracle. Such craft were probably the only ones known by humans for thousands of years.

Philippines, and Taiwan. They even moved over to Australia at least 45,000 years ago.

Earth's sea levels were much lower during much of this time. Some islands of today were linked by land. Australia and the islands mentioned, however, were separated by at least 50 miles (80 km) from the mainland. One theory, in fact, is that the *Homo sapiens* who moved from the Middle East to Southeast Asia during many thousands of years had done so by making short boat trips along the coasts. Whether they moved over land or sea, these early *Homo sapiens* were demonstrating courage, intelligence, and their commitment to moving into new territory.

THE FIRST AMERICANS

Nowhere was the commitment of *Homo sapiens* to adventurous travel more remarkable than in the migration of humans into the Western Hemisphere. Not all authorities agree on the time when these first humans appeared in North America, but it seems that it was at least about 16,000 B.C. This time was the last part of the great Ice Age. Much of Earth's water was "locked up" in huge ice caps and glaciers. These sheets of ice covered much of North America and northern Eurasia. The world's sea levels were so low that the land between Siberia and Alaska was exposed. It was by this route that the first humans entered North America. (Other authorities now believe that at least some of these first Americans made their way by boats from Asia to the western shores of North America.)

What is truly remarkable about the appearance of the first human beings in the Western Hemisphere is how fast they moved down and throughout the Americas. It has been calculated that human beings may have traveled the 10,000 miles (16,093 km) from the coast of Alaska to the tip of South America in 1,000 years. Although that would mean only 10 miles (16 km) a year, this was an amazing event in human history. People spread across two whole continents in a relatively short period of time.

The question then becomes: Why? What motivated these people to keep moving into unknown territories? Did they all have the spirit of explorers? This is hardly likely. More likely is that they were simply seeking better places to live. Drought conditions may often have played a role. More particularly, they were driven to seek food, for that was apparently the major if not their sole concern and occupation. These people subsisted almost entirely on hunting and food gathering. They hunted birds, fish, and large land animals. They gathered nuts, fruits, berries, roots, and many plants. In the competition for food, some of these people crowded out others. They needed to keep moving to stay alive.

The lifestyles and tools of the hunter-gatherers of North America were similar to those of other peoples of this period throughout the world. Most people still hunted wild animals and ranged widely in search of food sources. As widespread as human beings had become by about 10,000 B.C., however, the world was still quite sparsely inhabited. In most places, small bands of people roamed small areas. Most groups were extended families of up to 50 adults.

A CHANGING WORLD

About 10,000 B.C., the world began to change. The climate warmed rapidly. The great ice caps and glaciers were receding. New plant and animal species took over the land once dominated by the large animals. Whether because of this climate change or other causes such as the spread of disease pathogens and overhunting by humans, many of the world's large animals became extinct. In particular, those hunted in the Americas all became extinct. In Europe and Asia, woolly mammoths, rhinoceroses, cave bears, cave lions, Irish elk, large bison, and other giant species disappeared. The extinctions of animals in Africa did not proceed as rapidly, which may account in part for why sub-Saharan Africans at least did not feel the need to participate in the next major step in the development of human history—what is known as the Neolithic Revolution.

Neolithic means "new stone." The Neolithic Age did not begin at the same time and in the same way everywhere in the world, but in general, it was under way about 8000 B.C. By singling out stone, the term emphasizes that this period saw the development of a much more elaborate stone "toolkit." But the reason there were more specialized tools was that there were more specialized tasks to be accomplished. In fact, many of the tools were made from bone and antlers. Eventually some began to be made from metal such as copper. They began to make objects out of fibers—both baskets and textiles—and clay. They also began to domesticate animals such as sheep and cattle.

Perhaps the most significant development, however, was that people began to grow plants. This meant that people were settling down in more permanent settlements. As these settlements produced more reliable food, populations began to grow. The Neolithic Revolution marked

The bison pictured here was painted on the cave of Lascaux, in southwestern France, around 15,000 B.C. These prehistoric cave paintings feature nearly 2,000 realistic images of large animals, many of which are now extinct.

the beginning of village life and larger populations, which in turn would lead to the growth of cities.

By 3000 B.C., the world had changed greatly. Settlements, although still relatively scattered, now existed across much of the world. In addition to the lands already identified as inhabited, people kept moving into new places. Indeed, by 3000 B.C., it is easier to list the places on Earth where no one had yet set foot. Antarctica, of course, was an unknown continent. Many parts of the Arctic region also remained unexplored. The islands in the central Pacific region past the Philippines and New Guinea—including New Zealand—were still uninhabited. Large parts of the continental landmasses were empty of people. These included the Himalayan region, the Rocky Mountains, the highest Andes, and the largest deserts.

Still, by 3000 B.C., before any men or women known today as explorers even set out, most of the world had been discovered. Not inhabited, nor thoroughly explored. Nevertheless people had crossed bodies of water, climbed mountains, put up with extreme cold and heat, and faced fierce animals to move into unknown lands. Again the question arises: What caused people to move into so many faraway, even inhospitable lands?

As will be seen, even settling into large and comfortable cities does not destroy that desire. Along with the civilization that is almost defined by city life, there emerges the ability to write and record. With this skill, human beings embark on a new phase of discovery and exploration.

3

Early Ancient Explorers

THE FIRST SOCIETIES THAT WERE BASED IN CITIES AND THAT WOULD have the most influence on later Western history were those that emerged in the Near East and the eastern Mediterranean. The people from these cities traveled far into unknown lands and seas. These early explorers were not driven by some selfless desire to shed light on the unknown. Rather, most were engaged in trade or diplomacy or conquest. Some are credited today with being among the earliest of explorers.

THE SUMERIANS

The world's first major cities emerged between the Tigris and Euphrates rivers about 4000 B.C. This region is generally known as Mesopotamia, which means "between the rivers." For at least 3,500 years it was the homeland for a series of groups. The first of these were the Sumerians, a people of unknown origins who appeared in southern Mesopotamia and soon were developing a number of small but powerful city-states: Eridu, Kish, Lagash, Nippur, Umma, Ur, and Uruk. The Sumerians were the first people to develop a system of writing and were among the first to use wheeled vehicles. They were also active traders. In search of prized metals, stone, and wood, some of them went into the distant mountains of Armenia, the Taurus Mountains of Turkey, over into central Asia and Afghanistan, and even down into northern India. Others sailed out along the Persian Gulf. Some sailed as far south as the mouth of the Indus River in northwestern India and possibly west around the Arabian Peninsula as far as the Red Sea.

Sumerian writing is known as cuneiform. A sharp stylus was used to cut the letters into damp clay, leaving small impressions that were pointed at the interior and wider at the surface (like a wedge or a piece of pie). The clay was then baked to retain the writing, and many of the clay tablets have survived. The tablets contain records of many of the Sumerians' activities, but the names of the people who made journeys were usually not recorded.

Various poems and other writing from Mesopotamia of this era refer to distant lands. Most of the lands cannot be identified but it is clear that the Sumerians were aware of many products from faraway locales like Africa and Turkey. The great Sumerian emperor, Sargon of Akkad, allegedly left an account of a naval expedition that he led "across the sea in the west" and defeated Anaku-ki, Kapptara-ki, "and lands beyond the upper sea." Scholars debate just what these places were. Some claim Sargon of Akkad went as far as Spain. Others say he was referring to Cyprus and Crete. Still others say he never got beyond the Persian Gulf.

THE EGYPTIANS

Egypt emerged as a great power about 3200 B.C. For the most part, the lives of Egyptians were centered on the Nile River. Reed boats of all sizes moved up and down the river, carrying food and goods. Once the Egyptians began to make wooden boats, they realized that their land did not have enough trees. An inscribed stone (now in Palermo, Italy) describes how in about 2700 B.C. Egyptian Pharaoh Sneferu "brought 40 ships of cedar-wood" from Byblos, a Phoenician city on the Mediterranean. Sneferu also led a military expedition into the land south of Egypt known as Nubia.

Some 250 years later, an Egyptian named Harkhuf reported on his own journey to Nubia. He went there "to explore a road to this country. I did so in only seven months and I brought back gifts of all kinds ... 300 [mules] loaded with incense, ebony, grain, panthers, ivory, and every good product."

Several Egyptian pharaohs led military campaigns that took them into Mesopotamia, Syria, ancient Phoenicia (Lebanon), and Asia Minor (Turkey). The most famous expedition, however, was not a military campaign. It was a combination diplomatic and trade mission sponsored by Queen Hatshepsut, who ruled Egypt between about 1505 and 1485 B.C.

About 1492 B.C., she sent Egyptian ships down the Red Sea and into the Indian Ocean to what was called the Land of Punt. Punt may have been on the Horn of Africa or it may have been present-day India. This was not the first time Egyptians had visited the Land of Punt, but it was not until Hatshepsut's expedition that regular trade was maintained between the two lands.

Under Thutmose III, who ruled for some 30 years after Hatshepsut's death, Egypt expanded its power. It now controlled the entire eastern Mediterranean Coast and up into the northern reaches of the Tigris and Euphrates rivers. Egypt's southern borders extended down into Sudan and along the coast of the Red Sea. One of the aides to Thutmose III described how the pharaoh, after crossing the Euphrates River, moved into Syria and "hunted 120 elephants for the sake of their tusks."

The Sumerians were the first to develop a valid system of writing, known as cuneiform ("wedge-form"). A sharp instrument was used to cut letters into damp clay, which was then baked to retain the writing. The clay tablets, along with carvings like the one above, are a surviving record of the many activities of the Sumerians.

During this time, too, Egypt traded with peoples as far removed as Crete and Greece and possibly even Malta. Still, there is reason to believe that the Egyptians left much of the sailing to others. They stayed put in their own cities, letting foreigners do the sailing. The Egyptians, in fact, were not that interested in exploring past their circle of familiar trading partners.

MINOANS AND MYCENAEANS

One people who did move all across the Mediterranean Sea during this time were the Minoans. Between 2500 and 1500 B.C., they conducted a bustling commercial empire based on the island of Crete. Perhaps because Crete was relatively small—it is almost exactly the size of Puerto Rico—the people of Crete had always looked outward both to import goods and to export their own wares. Even before the emergence of the Minoan civilization—so named by modern archaeologists after a mythical Cretan king, Minos—Cretans were trading with Egypt; Minoans also traded with the island of Cyprus and other islands throughout the Aegean. There is some evidence to suggest that Minoans also sailed as far west as Italy and even Spain. In the east, Minoans seem to have had at least trade contacts with Turkey, Afghanistan, and India.

About 1500 B.C., Greeks from the mainland appear to have moved over to Crete and taken over from the Minoans. These Greeks, called Mycenaeans, also took over many of the Minoans' trade routes and contacts. The Mycenaeans were not all that interested in seeking out new lands or dominating foreign trade, however. This left the field open to some of the most adventurous people of the ancient world, the Phoenicians.

THE PHOENICIANS

The Phoenicians lived along the coasts of what are modern Syria, Lebanon, and Israel. Their name comes for the Greek word *phoinix*, meaning "red-purple," in recognition of the fact that these people were famous for trading in reddish-purple dyed goods, primarily textiles. Although considered backward when it came to institutional organization, the Phoenicians were among the most progressive of ancient peoples when it came to artful crafts, manufacturing, trade, and colonization. They also developed an alphabet that the Greeks and Romans borrowed and from which all Western alphabets have since been developed.

Considering that the Phoenicians had an alphabet and kept such careful records, it might seem strange that they did not leave accounts of their far-ranging voyages. The evidence, instead, comes from other peoples' accounts and from the physical remains that the Phoenicians left in many faraway places. The earliest record of Phoenician trade is the Egyptian account of the Pharaoh Sneferu's expedition to buy cedar wood from Byblos, a major Phoenician port city. Cedar and other trees would remain one of their major exports.

As early as 1200 B.C., the Phoenicians were some of the most important sailors in the eastern Mediterranean. The Phoenicians were soon founding colonies in the western Mediterranean—Utica in Tunisia, Gades (Cadiz) in Spain, Nora in Sardinia. The most famous of their colonies was Carthage, founded by Phoenicians on the coast of Tunisia about 800 B.C. Carthage soon became a major trading center and began to start its own colonies around the coast of Spain and on the Balearic Islands, on Sicily and Malta, and on Corsica and Sardinia. Although at first they do not seem to have resorted to force, the Carthaginians seemed determined to beat out their Greek rivals. By about 500 B.C., they had colonies on the North African coast opposite Gibraltar and so controlled traffic through the Strait of Gibraltar—the Pillars of Hercules to the Greeks.

Once the Carthaginians were solidly established at the far end of the Mediterranean, they decided to journey out into the Atlantic. There are two major expeditions by Carthaginians. One of these was led by Himilco, who sailed into the Atlantic as far as the French coast of Brittany around 500 B.C. He may have sailed as far as Cornwall, on the southwestern tip of Britain, reached some 200 years later by Pytheas. He may even have sailed far out into the North Atlantic as far as the Sargasso Sea, well past the Azores. Such extreme claims are rejected by most scholars, however, so everything about Himilco's voyage remains questionable.

A somewhat more solid story involves another Carthaginian, Hanno. He posted an account of his voyage at a temple in Carthage when he returned. It is that account that is quoted by Polybius, a Greek historian of the second century B.C.:

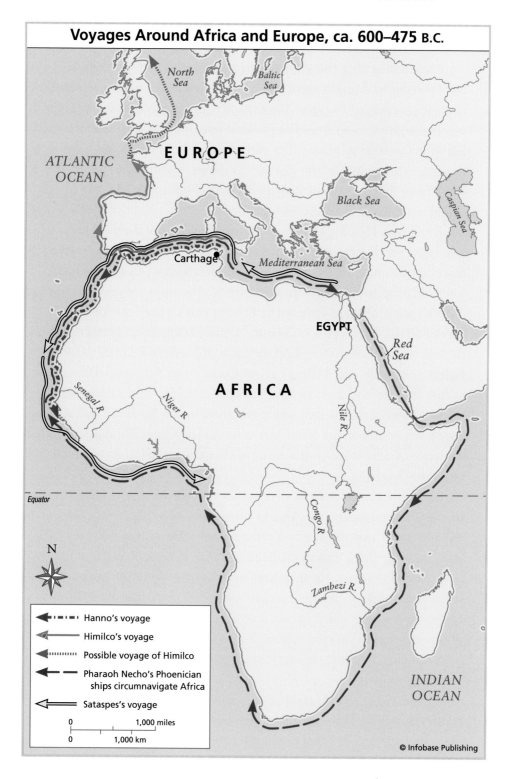

Voyages Around Africa and Europe, ca. 600–475 B.C.

North Sea

Baltic Sea

EUROPE

ATLANTIC OCEAN

Black Sea

Caspian Sea

Carthage

Mediterranean Sea

EGYPT

Red Sea

Senegal R.

Niger R.

AFRICA

Nile R.

Equator

N

Congo R.

Zambezi R.

INDIAN OCEAN

◄–·–·– Hanno's voyage

◄——— Himilco's voyage

◄········· Possible voyage of Himilco

◄– – – Pharaoh Necho's Phoenician ships circumnavigate Africa

◄═══ Sataspes's voyage

0		1,000 miles
0	1,000 km	

© Infobase Publishing

He set sail with sixty vessels of fifty oars and a multitude of men and women to the number of 30,000 and provisions and other equipment. After putting out to sea and passing the Pillars [of Hercules] we sailed beyond them for two days.

At this point, Hanno, unlike Himilco, turned south and proceeded down the northwest coast of Africa:

We sailed on for half a day until we arrived at a lagoon full of high and thick-grown cane. This was haunted by elephants and multitudes of other grazing beasts.

Continuing down along the coast, Hanno went ashore at various points and reported all manner of exotic sights:

Beyond these dwelt inhospitable Ethiopians [Africans]. Their land is infested with wild beasts. . . . These highlands are inhabited by a freakish race of men, the Troglodytes [from Greek for "hole dwellers," here referring to some unknown African people] who are said to run faster than horses. . . . Sailing on from that point we came to another deep and wide river, which was infested with crocodiles and hippopotami. . . . The second island was full of wild people. By far the greater number were women with hairy bodies. Our interpreters called them Gorillas.

There are many questions raised by Hanno's voyage. The major question is just how far down the coast of Africa he went. Some scholars say he got no farther than Morocco, on the northwestern shoulder. Some say he got all the way to Sierra Leone, only eight degrees above the equator. If this is true, Hanno was 3,000 miles (4,828 km) from Carthage, making for a round-trip almost as ambitious as that of Columbus's. It would be 2,000 years before any European got as far down the coast of Africa.

(opposite page) This map shows the routes Hanno and Himilco sailed on their voyages around Africa. Modern scholars disagree on how far they actually traveled. Because the ancient explorers did not have the equipment needed to measure accurately, there were many distortions and errors.

The Phoenicians sailed to many other places. Some scholars are convinced that they even reached the Americas. The supporters of this theory point to inscriptions they claim to be in the Phoenician language and other finds such as coins. Most serious scholars reject all such claims.

One story of a major Phoenician journey, however, has been the subject of debate almost since the time it was first reported. That is the voyage sponsored by the Egyptian pharaoh Necho about 600 B.C. The only account of this story is from the ancient Greek historian Herodotus. He describes the journey:

> *Africa is clearly surrounded by water except where it touches Asia. Necho, pharaoh of Egypt, was the first person we know of to demonstrate this. After he had finished digging out a canal between the Nile and the Red Sea, he sent out a naval expedition manned by Phoenicians, instructing them to come back by entering the Mediterranean through the Pillars of Hercules and in that way return to Egypt. Setting out from the Red Sea, the Phoenicians sailed into the Indian Ocean. Each autumn they put in at whatever part of Africa they happened to be sailing by; there they planted crops and stayed until harvest time, reaped the grain, and then sailed on. In that way, two years passed and it was not until the third year that they entered the Pillars of Hercules and made their way back to Egypt. They reported many things that others can believe if they choose to, but I cannot—in particular, that while sailing around Africa they had the sun on their right side.*

Most scholars find it hard to accept that any sailor at this time sailed around Africa at such an early point in history; however, they agree that it could be done. These sailors could have had favorable weather. They could have put ashore for several months to grow a crop of grain. The very detail Herodotus singles out as disproving such a story actually supports it. If the sailors had rounded the tip of Africa, the sun would often have been to the north—that is, to their right.

In the end, the Phoenicians—for all their initiative and ambition when it came to sailing, colonizing, and trading—showed little interest in exploring for the sake of discovering the unknown or of adding to the sum of their contemporaries' knowledge.

THE PERSIANS

About the time when the Phoenicians' empire was at its strongest, a new power rose up in the Middle East. The Persians lived in the lands

FICTITIOUS EXPLORATIONS

Separating fact from fiction is hard to do in the study of ancient exploration. People in these times often did not have the means to observe, to measure, and to record "facts" about their world. Information was passed on largely by word of mouth, and this inevitably led to errors and distortions. In addition, ancient peoples placed great faith in myths and legends. They were not anxious to displace these with scientific evidence. It is no wonder, then, that some of the earliest stories about discovery and exploration are probably fictional accounts.

A famous Babylonian poem, for instance, tells the story of Gilgamesh. He was said to have been a powerful and oppressive ruler. Gilgamesh defeated groups in southern Mesopotamia and traveled into the southern Arabian Peninsula. He then crossed the Arabian Sea and went on to Somaliland in Africa. Although the best surviving copy of this epic dates to only the seventh century B.C., it is known to include myths, folklore, and tales dating back to well before 2000 B.C. Although clearly fictional, the poem served to introduce the Babylonians to a world beyond their narrow confines.

The Egyptians, meanwhile, told a story of a merchant who was sent on a business trip by a pharaoh. When his ship was wrecked in a storm, he alone survived and was washed up on an island. The merchant was rescued by a ship that a giant snake had loaded with fine products to bring back to Egypt. The story was written down on a papyrus as early as 2000 B.C. and seems to be describing a journey to the Land of Punt variously located in India, Africa, or Arabia.

known today as Iran and Afghanistan. By 549 B.C., the Persians controlled territory from the Mediterranean Coast all the way to what is now Pakistan. Led by their king, Cyrus the Great, the Persians controlled the Phoenicians' own homeland as well as Mesopotamia, and Cyrus's successors would extend Persian power still farther—including parts of northern Greece, Egypt, and Libya.

They ruled this huge empire with a relatively light hand, allowing most peoples to continue in their own ways. They could retain their languages, religions, and cultures. The Persians were more interested in trade and taxes. They encouraged caravans to cross their land, exchanging wares between Europe and Asia. The Persians also built a network of roads connecting their major cities. Although their ships sailed all around the Persian Gulf and the Arabian Sea, they were a land-based empire. Persia looked more to the east than to the west.

Unfortunately, almost none of the Persians' own accounts of their discoveries survive. Herodotus, however, described an important expedition sponsored by the Persian emperor Darius, who ruled from 521–486 B.C.

> *The greater part of Asia was explored by Darius, who desired to know more about the Indus River, which is one of the two rivers in the world to produce crocodiles. He wanted to know where this river runs out onto the sea and sent in ships both those on whom he could rely to make a true report and also Scylax of Caryanda.*
>
> *They set out from the city of Caspatyrus in the land of Pacty-ike, sailed down the river toward the east and to the sea. Sailing westward over the sea, they came in the thirtieth month to the place from where the king of the Egyptians had sent out the Phoenicians of whom I have spoken earlier [the expedition of Necho] to sail around Africa.*

What is interesting is that Scylax was Greek. His home city, Caryanda, was under Persian rule. His role in this expedition thus confirms the sense that the Persians were open to foreigners.

Scylax, by the way, was so respected in his day that a periplus, or sailing guide, was attributed to him, even though it clearly was composed at least two centuries later—about 350 B.C. The book was the *Periplus of*

Scylax. It was an amazingly detailed guide to the many islands, rivers, harbors, towns, and even peoples of the region. It described the waters connecting these places and the distances between them. It is so thorough that many people believe that what has survived to this day is a work that was corrected over the years.

Another famous Persian expedition was led by a cousin of the Emperor Xerxes (who ruled from 485–465 B.C.). Once again, the only source for this story is Herodotus. He told how Sataspes was to be put to death for a crime when his mother persuaded Xerxes to send him on a trip to circumnavigate, or sail around, Africa. Sataspes sailed in the opposite direction from the one taken by Necho. He sailed west through the Strait of Gibraltar and down along the northwestern coast of Africa. Herodotus went on:

> *After sailing for many months over a vast amount of water and always finding he had to go further, he turned around and made his way back to Egypt. From there he returned to Xerxes and reported that, at the farthest point he reached, he sailed by a dwarf race who wore clothes of palm leaves and fled their villages to the mountains whenever Sataspes and his men went ashore, and that he and his men did them no harm but only went in and took some cattle. But finally, the reason he didn't sail all around Africa was that the ship stopped and just could not go any further.*

Upon hearing this excuse for failing to complete his task, Xerxes had Sataspes killed after all. Whether true or not, such a tale perhaps says something about the risks assumed by early explorers.

A number of Greeks have begun to play important roles in the history of exploration by this time—Herodotus, Scylax, Alexander the Great. This is no coincidence. The Persian Empire was about to be challenged by the Greeks, who would bring a whole new dimension to exploration.

4

The Inquisitive Greeks

THE PEOPLE KNOWN TODAY AS THE ANCIENT GREEKS NEVER CALLED themselves that. They call themselves "Hellenes," just as they call their country "Hellas." In ancient times, they referred to themselves by the name of the major city-state in which they lived or which dominated their region. (City-states were forms of government centered around major cities.) There were Athenians, Corinthians, Spartans, and so on. What makes their story so amazing, then, is the way these disparate groups managed to shape and share a culture that was so distinctive. In particular, the Greeks showed a modern interest about the world at large.

THE EARLY HISTORY OF THE GREEKS

People had been living on the Greek mainland and islands for thousands of years. The first people who could be called Greeks came to these lands from somewhere to the north about the year 2000 B.C. Little is known of them except that they spoke an Indo-European language that was the ancestor of classical and modern Greek. They worshipped a number of gods, among whom a male deity was supreme, and behaved in a relatively aggressive manner. They became known as Achaeans. Within a few centuries, they were the dominant people in much of Greece. By about 1650 B.C., they had settled Mycenae in the southern part of Greece. Mycenae emerged as the most powerful of the Achaean settlements. Because of this, the Achaeans are also known as Mycenaeans.

Although not primarily a seagoing people, the Mycenaeans made their presence felt around the Mediterranean. By about 1500 B.C., they moved over to Crete and took control of the island's centers and economy from the Minoans. They moved on to Cyprus and the southern coast of Turkey. They even founded settlements in Syria. Meanwhile, they also sailed to the west, trading with the people of southern Italy, Sicily, Sardinia, and possibly even Spain. The Mycenaeans did not set forth to find new lands. They traveled the well-known routes of the day, apparently interested solely in trade.

By about 1150 B.C., a new wave of Greek-speaking people moved down from the north and began to compete with the Mycenaeans. These people were known as Dorians. Within a century or two, they had replaced the Mycenaeans as the dominant people in many parts of Greece. They had also moved onto Crete, Rhodes, southwestern Asia Minor (Turkey), Sicily, and southern Italy. The Dorians were even less of a seagoing people than the Mycenaeans and do not seem to have taken over any new lands.

It was a third group of people—the Ionians—who seem to have brought the most adventurous and innovative streak to the mix known as "the Greeks." No one knows exactly where the Ionians came from but whoever they were, they appear to have spoken a language close to that of the Achaeans and the Dorians. When the Dorians moved down across Greece about 1000 B.C., some Ionians apparently fled to Attica, the region where Athens is located, while others fled to the southwestern coast of Turkey. The Ionians who settled on the coast and islands of Turkey would become so prosperous and prominent that they would eventually take the lead over mainland Greeks in various endeavors.

SHARED STORIES

By about 800 B.C., a single culture was growing in Greece. The culture the people themselves would call "Hellenic" was based on such elements as the common language, particular techniques and motifs in their arts and crafts, and certain ways of arranging their social, economic, and political systems. Above all, these ancient Greeks shared myths, legends, and tales that expressed their views of the world and humans' relations with it. The Greeks told these stories as though they were part of their history. Some stories told of heroes who did amazing things.

Athens felt it was first among equals and demonstrated it by constructing its great temple, the Parthenon (447–438 B.C.), and other fine buildings. Athens was the greatest cultural center of its time. (In the foreground is the Odeon of Herodes Atticus, a theater erected by a wealthy Roman in the late second century A.D.)

Perhaps the best known of these heroes was Herakles (or Hercules, as he was known to the Romans).

One of the common themes of the stories of these heroes is that they traveled far and wide around the Mediterranean. They even went outside its bounds to perform their deeds. Of course, these tales were mythological, meaning they were imaginative. Still, Greek heroic myths express the Greeks' willingness both to seek out new lands and to communicate information, however incorrect.

This was especially true with the story of Jason. Jason led an expedition of 50 men in search of the Golden Fleece. Their ship was named the *Argo,* so the men were known as the Argonauts. The Golden Fleece came from a ram, or male goat, that had been sacrificed to the god Zeus. It hung from a grove of trees in Colchis, a distant land at the far eastern end of the Black Sea. After sailing there and obtaining the fleece, Jason and the Argonauts made their way back to Greece. This story, like those of the other heroes, was full of fictional doings. Scholars cannot agree on exactly what real places were being referred to. However, some Greeks had made their way up to the Black Sea by at least 800 B.C. and by 700 B.C., they were setting up the first of many colonies in that area.

The best known of the stories of the ancient Greeks were Homer's epic poems, *The Iliad* and *The Odyssey.* Almost nothing is known of Homer, although it is generally believed that he came from one of the Ionian cities along the coast of present-day Turkey. It is also believed that he wrote down these poems about 750 B.C. Whoever he was, it is quite certain that a large portion of the poems attributed to Homer had been passed along for several centuries by generations of storytellers.

The Iliad tells the story of the Trojan War and is largely confined to the locale of Troy. *The Odyssey,* however, tells the story of the 10-year voyage of Odysseus's attempts to make his way home after the Trojan War. Along the way, he has many adventures at various exotic locales. People try to identify the places he visited with sites around the Mediterranean. Some believe he traveled well outside that sea—as far as Britain. Others place his journey in the Black Sea. *The Odyssey* is the greatest example of the ancient Greeks' love of exploration. It is no wonder that young Greeks raised on *The Odyssey* wanted to set out to see the world.

THE IONIANS

Until about 650 B.C., people on Earth chose to explain the world, both known and unknown, by myths, legends, and other imaginative accounts. About then, however, some Greeks began using science and mathematics to account for Earth and its phenomena. Most of them were Ionian Greeks who lived along the coast of Turkey and its offshore islands. Thales, who lived from about 640–546 B.C., used geometry to predict an eclipse of the sun—an event that most people attributed to the gods. About 550 B.C., Anaximander claimed that the entire universe was a sphere, with Earth at the center and the moon, planets, stars, and sun encircling it. He also drew the first map of Earth.

Hecataeus came along about 500 B.C. and improved Anaximander's map by adding more details. It is also said that Hecataeus wrote two volumes, *Europe* and *Asia*, described as "a journey round the world." Although he gained the title "Father of Geography," the books do not prove that Hecataeus traveled widely. They do not even mean that he had a solid knowledge of Earth. In fact, he believed, like most Greeks, that there were only two continents. Africa was regarded as part of Asia. Also, although Hecataeus thought of Earth as round, he regarded it as a flat plane, with the two continents surrounded by an ocean.

These individuals had apparently arrived at these versions of Earth by collecting information that was brought to them by others and using mathematics and other mental calculations. Much of the information came from sailors, traders, and colonists who traveled to distant lands. The port city of Phocaea (near the modern Turkish village of Foca) was among the leaders in trade. During the 500s B.C., it founded a string of trading stations along the Mediterranean coast, from southern Italy to Spain. Some of the Phocaean settlements grew into wealthy cities. Massalia, the home of Pytheas, the mariner credited with sailing northwestern Europe, was the best known of these. The Phocaeans also founded settlements along both shores of the Adriatic Sea, between eastern Italy and Yugoslavia. The Greeks who went off to establish these settlements may not have been heroes like the Argonauts. They were probably motivated primarily by the desire to improve their own lot in life.

OTHER GREEKS, OTHER JOURNEYS

Ionians were not the only Greeks active in exploring distant lands between 650 and 400 B.C. Scylax has already been mentioned. He was the mariner hired by the Persian king Darius to lead an expedition to India and the Persian Gulf. Scylax was from Caria, a region just south of the Ionian Greek region (in southwestern Turkey). If not a Greek himself, he was probably influenced by the Ionian Greeks. There was even the story that another citizen of Caria, Euphemus, was blown by the winds through the Strait of Gibraltar. He traveled all across the great ocean to an island inhabited by red-skinned men with horses' tails.

Some people claim that this shows that he got all the way to the Antilles (in the Caribbean); however, no scholars accept this.

Herodotus, the Greek historian, told of a sailor named Colaeus. In about 640 B.C., Colaeus was trying to sail from the coast of North Africa back to his island home of Samos, off the coast of Turkey. Heavy winds instead blew him west all the way across the Mediterranean and outside the Strait of Gibraltar to the land of Tartessus on the southwestern coast of Spain. There Colaeus is said to have picked up such a large load of silver that, when he got back to Samos, he was able to retire.

Then there was a tale about a certain sea captain from Massalia, the same Greek colony that was the home port to Pytheas. The captain supposedly wrote a periplus, or guide to coastal settlements, about 525 B.C. In this periplus, the Massalian sailor shows a good knowledge of the coast of Spain. He also refers to the British Isles and even to Ireland. There was still another Massalian, Euthymenes, who about 530 B.C. was said to have sailed through the Strait of Gibraltar and down along the west coast of Africa. There he came to a large river in which he saw crocodiles, which Euthymenes believed indicated he had seen the Upper Nile.

Nothing about these tales can be verified, but what matters is the message between the lines. The Greeks knew the risks of setting out to sea, yet they were intrigued by the prospects of traveling far from home.

TWO ADVENTUROUS GREEKS

Perhaps no one represented this spirit of the ancient Greeks more than Herodotus. Born about 484 B.C., he traveled widely in his youth. He visited parts of Greece, Mesopotamia, the Phoenician coast, Egypt, the eastern coast of North Africa, and even southwest Russia. He visited Athens in 447 B.C., and by 443 B.C. he had moved to a new Greek colony in southern Italy. He was writing a history of the world up to his time, with emphasis on the wars between the Persians and the Greeks (499–479 B.C.). But Herodotus's history was much more than what is understood by that word today. In addition to the historical narrative, it is an encyclopedia of geographical facts gained firsthand or from his research. It includes observations on groups of people, quotations from major writers and obscure sources, and stories.

Herodotus was called "the Father of History" by the great Greek philosopher Aristotle, but he might also be called the first true explorer. Almost no person earlier than Herodotus had such curiosity

LOST ATLANTIS

One of the most lasting contributions of the ancient Greeks to the discovery of new lands is fiction: the tale of Lost Atlantis. The story began with the famous Greek philosopher Plato (429–347 B.C.), who in two of his works, the *Timaeus* and the *Critias,* told of a story allegedly passed on to Greeks by an Egyptian priest. He said Atlantis had existed 9,000 years before ancient Athens. The island was located in the great ocean outside the Pillars of Hercules—that is, the Strait of Gibraltar.

Atlantis was a highly advanced and wealthy land. It had quantities of gold, ambitious canals, plentiful fruits and flowers, great palaces, a horse-racing track, and wild bulls that were hunted down. Atlantis was purportedly the center of an empire that dominated much of the Mediterranean world until Athens rose up and defeated it. After that, violent earthquakes and floods overwhelmed Atlantis, and in one day the whole island sank to the depths of the ocean. Most of the ancients recognized Plato's story as fiction intended to teach a lesson: The pursuit of too much wealth and power was bad for society.

With the Europeans' discovery of the Americas, however, Atlantis suddenly emerged as though it were a real place. People believed many places in the Americas were Atlantis. Somehow the fact that Atlantis was to have sunk beneath the waves was overlooked.

Today, a new twist has been added to this story. Actual expeditions—some costing large sums of money and involving professional scientists—set forth to points all over the world to search for Atlantis. Every few years another "explorer" claims to have found the actual remains of Atlantis. So it is that this ancient Greek tale has stimulated centuries of discussions that have contributed in some degree to exploring and revealing disputed parts of the world.

about the world at large. He gathered every bit of information he could about the places he visited and those he was only told about. Many of the stories about the early explorers are known only because Herodotus wrote them. Many places in distant parts—southwest Russia, for example, or lower Egypt—were barely known about until Herodotus reported on them.

Here is Herodotus telling of how he learned much about Egypt from the priests he met at Egyptian temples:

> *Those of their narrations that I heard with regard to the gods, I am not anxious to relate in full, but I shall mention them only because I consider that all men are equally ignorant of these matters: and whatever things of them I may record I shall record only because I am compelled by the course of the story. [The priests] said also that the first man who became king of Egypt was Min; and that in his time all Egypt except the district of Thebes was a swamp, and none of the regions were then above water which now lie below the lake of Moiris, to which lake it is a voyage of seven days up the river from the sea. I thought that they said well about the land, for it is manifestly true even to a person who has not heard it beforehand but has only seen, at least if he have understanding, that the Egypt to which the Hellenes come in ships is a land that has been won by the Egyptians as an addition, and that it is a gift of the river.*

After talking with the priests, like a true explorer he set out to learn about the source of the Nile and its annual flooding. He eventually concluded: "[A]bout the sources of the Nile, no one, whether Egyptian or Libyan or Greek, who has talked with me, has admitted that he knew anything, except the clerk of the holy utensil at the shrine of Athene in Sais in Egypt; but I think he was joking when he said he knew accurately."

Herodotus died about 424 B.C. Just a few years before his death, in about 430 B.C., another remarkable Greek was born. Xenophon was an Athenian aristocrat and military man. In 401 B.C., he accepted an invitation from the Persian Cyrus the Younger to join a military campaign that turned out to be an attempt to overthrow Cyrus's older brother,

In writing the *Anabasis*, Athenian military leader Xenophon introduced a whole new region to his fellow Greeks. The realistic account of his epic trek across the Middle East was different from the mythological tales the ancient peoples were used to.

Artaxerxes, king of Persia. After Cyrus was killed in the battle, Xenophon assumed command of the Greek army and led them on their retreat from the Persians. Their six-month journey took them some 800 miles (1,287 km) from near Baghdad all the way to the Black Sea. They often had to fight off hostile forces. It was an epic feat that might have gone unnoticed had not Xenophon eventually written a stirring account of it, the *Anabasis*. The title is often translated as "The Retreat of the 10,000."

After the army made its way north out of Mesopotamia, they moved across the regions known today as Kurdistan and Turkish Armenia. It appears that they reached the source of the Tigris River and passed near the source of the Euphrates. During the winter weeks, they found themselves in the rugged mountains. Many died from the cold and exhaustion. Finally they arrived at a mountain peak. Xenophon described this event in one of the best known passages in Greek history:

No sooner had the men in the lead ascended it and caught sight of the sea than a great cry arose. Xenophon, in the rear, catching the sound of it, assumed that another group of enemies must be attacking. . . . But as the shout became louder and nearer, and those who from time to time came up from the rear began racing at full speed toward the shouting, and the shouting continued at still greater volume as the numbers increased, Xenophon

*realized that something extraordinary must have occurred, so
he mounted his horse and taking his cavalry with him, galloped
to the rescue. Presently they could hear the soldiers shouting and
passing on the joyful word, "The sea! The sea!"*

Xenophon never saw himself as an explorer. He wrote his account
as a historian, but he was so observant and so graphic that his *Anabasis*
served to introduce a whole new region to his fellow Greeks. Consider a
typical passage from the *Anabasis*. The Greeks have captured a group of
men in northern Mesopotamia and are wondering what lies ahead:

*After hearing the statements of the prisoners, the Greek officers
seated apart those who claimed to have any special knowledge of
the country in any direction. They sat them apart without making it clear which particular route they intended to take. Finally
they decided that they must force a passage through the hills into
the territory of the Kurds; according to what their informants
told them, when they had once passed these, they would find
themselves in Armenia—the rich and large territory governed by
Orontas—and from Armenia it would be easy to proceed in any
direction. Thereupon they offered sacrifice so as to be ready to
start on the march as soon as the right moment arrived. Their
chief fear was that the high pass over the mountains might be
occupied in advance.*

This is a far cry from the mythological versions of adventures and
exotic lands that most ancient peoples were used to.

THE GREEKS' LIMITED KNOWLEDGE

At the same time that Xenophon was fighting alongside Cyrus, another
Greek was aiding Cyrus's brother, King Artaxerxes. This was Ctesias,
a physician from Cnidos, a Greek colony on the southwest coast of
Turkey. Little is known about Ctesias, and none of his writings have
survived in their original texts. It is clear from other ancient authors
that he was famed for a history of India that he had written. Ctesias's
so-called history was hardly what would be called history today. It was

clearly little more than a collection of tales that he heard while at the Persian court.

Another ancient writer, Dionysus of Halicarnassus, called Ctesias's work "entertaining but badly composed." Ctesias did not claim to have visited India, and the land he describes is full of the exotic and fabulous, although it is possible that some of what he claims is based on misunderstandings. For instance, Ctesias says that in India there dwells some people who have only one very large foot, a foot so big they can use it as a sunshade. Some scholars suggest that Ctesias simply misunderstood reports of the practice of certain Indian holy men who stood in unusual poses for a long time, usually on one foot.

Ctesias is an extreme example of the Greeks' misconceptions of the world. There is no denying, however, that most ancient Greeks' descriptions of the world were full of errors. They traveled and researched, yet they simply did not know enough about the world beyond their own lands, primarily the lands surrounding the Mediterranean Sea. This would change with the contributions of the man who came to be known as Alexander the Great.

5

Alexander the Great and the Hellenistic World

FOR ALL THEIR ACCOMPLISHMENTS, THE ANCIENT GREEKS WERE IN fact limited in their knowledge of the world at large. Partly this was because it was not that easy to learn about the world beyond one's immediate region. A ship captain might return from some distant land and describe unusual sights, but such tales would not have carried far. Partly, too, it was because the ancient Greeks had a certain smugness, a sense of superiority. They felt they had the most civilized and the most sophisticated society. There was no great need to rush off to seek out new places. This is reflected in their word for non-Greek speakers—*barbaros.* Believed to be derived from the sound of the languages spoken by non-Greeks, it meant foreign, crude, and ignorant. The Greeks believed there was not much to be gained from "barbarians."

North of the Greek city-states was a vast territory known as Macedon. This land is now divided up among Greece, the Republic of Macedonia, and Bulgaria. A raw, mountainous land, most of it was as shadowy as its inhabitants. Even today, scholars are not absolutely clear about just who the ancient Macedonians were—that is, their ethnic origins and relationships. The ancient Greeks just tended to regard them as, at least, semibarbarians.

Although Macedon long remained a rather primitive society compared to the great city-states of Greece, many Macedonians spoke a form of Greek and their leaders claimed to share Greek culture. When Philip II took over the throne of Macedon in 359 B.C., he asserted his "Greekness" by setting about to conquer the Greek city-states. By 336, he had accomplished this and was preparing to lead an invasion of Persia when he was killed. His 20-year-old son, Alexander, took over the throne. Alexander accomplished so much that he would go down in history as one of the few individuals always identified as "the great." Although this usually is taken to refer to his military feats, the case can be made that the same word characterizes his role in the history of exploration.

ALEXANDER THE WARRIOR

Many of the tales told of Alexander were of the legendary kind, but there was probably at least a grain of truth behind them. For instance, it was claimed that when he heard about his father's conquests of the Greek city-states, he cried, saying, "My father will leave nothing great for me to do." He was said to have carried a copy of Homer's *Iliad* with him at all times because he so admired the warrior-hero Achilles. It was also said that his favorite horse, Bucephalus, was one that no one else had dared to try to tame.

When he was 13 years old, Alexander's parents hired the Greek philosopher Aristotle to tutor him. Aristotle knew as much as any person at that time. He taught Alexander the great classics and ideals of Greek culture. He also taught him about the countries and peoples elsewhere in the known world, as well as the natural history about plants and animals. By the time he became king, then, Alexander was not only a brave young man, he was an intelligent and curious one.

Among his first acts as king were to extend his rule over some of the tribes north of Macedonia and to put down a revolt in the Greek city-state of Thebes. He then sold most of its 30,000 citizens into slavery. After this, the rest of the Greek city-states, including Athens, acknowledged Alexander's leadership. By the spring of 334 B.C., he was ready to pursue the goal his father had in mind before he was killed—to conquer the Persian Empire.

(opposite page) Alexander the Great succeeded his father, Philip II, king of Macedonia, at the age of 20. Alexander became one of the most successful military leaders of all time. His success gave rise to the Hellenistic Age, a period of openness to new ideas and places that resulted from the diversity of peoples and cultures within his empire.

Over the next four years, with an army made up of 35,000 Macedonians, Greeks, and foreign mercenaries, Alexander led his often-outnumbered troops in a series of battles. He conquered all the major cities of the Persian Empire, including the Phoenician port city of Tyre (in modern Lebanon), the Egyptian city of Memphis, and the Mesopotamian city of Babylon (in modern Iraq). He even conquered and burned the Persian capital city of Persepolis (in modern Iran). While in Egypt, he founded the first of many cities he would establish, the city of Alexandria, along the Mediterranean coast. It would become one of the great cities of the ancient world.

ALEXANDER THE EXPLORER

Alexander's original mission was complete. Alexander released the many Greeks who wanted to go home, which says something about the Greeks' attitude toward the world at large. They had now traversed the world that they knew about; beyond lay the unknown—and these Greeks were not interested in exploring this "barbarian" world. Alexander was still interested in exploring, and during the next five years he led a mixed army of Macedonians and mercenaries from several lands in one of the most amazing expeditions of all time.

True, Alexander's immediate goal was to conquer more lands. Yet, he must have been motivated by something beyond the mere desire to win battles and acquire territory. In any case, the expedition earns its place in the history of exploration because Alexander—faithful to his tutor, Aristotle—took along a number of scientists to observe and record all that was new.

Alexander took with him some *bematists* (Greek for "pacers"), meaning surveyors, who measured the distances of the routes. They also recorded the peoples and products along the way. Much of the land they visited was inhabited. Still, this was an expedition of discovery because the reports of Alexander's staff brought this vast region of Asia into the consciousness of the Western world.

Alexander set out from Persepolis in the spring of 330 B.C. He led his army north into the region known as Media. He then moved along the southern shore of the Caspian Sea eastward through Parthia. After turning down into southeastern Persia, he headed north into Afghanistan.

At one point he crossed a mountain pass at 8,700 feet (2,651 meters), where his troops suffered greatly from the cold and snow.

Alexander's army spent the winter in northern Afghanistan (near the location of modern Kabul). It set out again in the spring of 329 B.C. and crossed the mountain range known as the Hindu Kush. It entered regions known as Bactria and Sogdiana. After crossing the great river Jaxartes (now the Syr Darya), Alexander founded a city. It marked the farthest point he reached in central Asia.

In the spring of 327 B.C., Alexander set out for India. One part of his army entered India through what is now the famous Khyber Pass. Alexander led another group through the mountains. This land was so wild that it would be another 2,220 years before there was any record of an explorer visiting them. He joined up with his other troops on the banks of the Indus River (in what is now Pakistan). The army rested over the winter before crossing over into the region known as the Punjab. There, in spring 326 B.C., Alexander led his troops against the Fortress of Aornus, high on a rock. In a seemingly impossible feat, Alexander defeated the Indian tribesmen who had taken refuge there. He then proceeded to defeat the most powerful prince in northwestern India. His beloved horse, Bucephalus, died after this battle. Alexander founded the city of Bucephala on the site.

Alexander intended to march further south and conquer more of India, but his troops refused to go any farther. Alexander had his men build a small fleet of ships. With about half his troops marching along both sides of the Indus River and the rest in the ships, he led his army to the Arabian Sea. Along the way, they were amazed by some of the exotic plants they saw. One of his companions, Onesicritus, described the great banyan trees in his account of the trip:

> *The branches . . . grow downwards until they touch the earth; after which they spread underground and take root like layers and then spring up and grow into a stem; after that again . . . they are bent down and form first one and then another layer, and so on continuously so that from one tree proceeds a long sunshade, resembling a tent supported by many poles, . . . the trees are of such a size that five men can with difficulty clasp their trunks.*

The Khyber Pass on the border of Afghanistan and Pakistan has been an important trade route between central and south Asia since ancient times. Alexander the Great led one part of his army through this pass—which cuts through the Safed Koh Mountains—for his entry into northern India.

Alexander needed to get his men back to Babylon, the city he had chosen to be the capital of his new empire in Asia. He sent one section of his army across western India and southern Persia (Iran). He divided his remaining forces into two groups. He led one group westward overland. The other stayed with the ships they had built to sail down the Indus. This fleet, commanded by a Cretan-Greek admiral, Nearchus, sailed along the coasts of the Arabian Sea and the Persian Gulf until reaching the mouth of the Euphrates River. Nearchus sailed some 1,400 miles (2,253 km) through largely unknown waters and along an unknown coast. This expedition ranks as one of the great voyages of the ancient world.

Many of Nearchus's detailed descriptions of the places he visited can be easily assigned to known places today. He also described many unusual encounters during the five months they were either sailing or seeking food and water onshore. At one point, they had to fight off some 600 "savages." Nearchus described those they took captive:

> They were hairy over their heads as well as the rest of their persons and had fingernails like wild beasts; at least they were said to use their nails like iron tools and to kill fish by tearing with them and to cut up woods of the softer sorts. . . . For clothing they wore the skins of wild beasts, some indeed wearing the thick skins of the bigger fish.

Nearchus and his crew eventually sailed up to the head of the Persian Gulf and made their way up the Tigris River. He soon rejoined Alexander, who had journeyed across southern Persia and into Mesopotamia. His trip, which had taken about the same five months, had its own challenges. He also traveled through uncharted and rugged territory, aggravated by the extreme heat and constant shortages of food and water. He had lost thousands of men along the way. Thousands of others had chosen to stay behind. Eventually, Alexander reached Babylon in early 324 B.C.

ALEXANDER'S LEGACY

It had been a truly fabulous six years since Alexander had set out from Persepolis. These were years in which he won many major battles. He founded 70 outposts and cities. He also overcame the most difficult physical obstacles imaginable. The writings of his companions would throw light on a part of Earth that had been consigned to darkness.

Alexander set about bringing order to his huge empire. He also planned other expeditions, but before he could continue with his explorations, he died of malaria in June 323 B.C. Alexander left behind one son, but he was only an infant, so Alexander's generals shared in governing the empire. They fought so much, however, that by 311 B.C., they split up the empire into three kingdoms.

Not only had Alexander established those many outposts and cities, he had set up Greek and Macedonian rulers in much of the territory that he had conquered. Many of his Greek and Macedonian soldiers had stayed behind to make new lives in these distant lands. The Greek

Empire of Alexander the Great, 334–323 B.C.

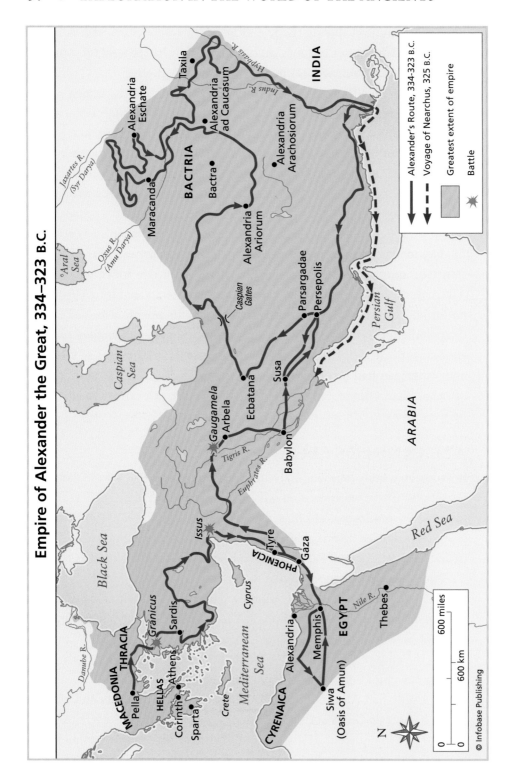

language, Greek culture, and Greek commerce were used now through-out these lands. This phase of history is known as the Hellenistic Age, named for the Greeks who called themselves "Hellenes." This age lasted until the Romans took over most of this realm about 200 years later.

The Hellenistic Age was characterized by the spread of Greek ideas and culture. There was also an openness to new ideas, new places, and new ways of doing things. Pytheas, the Greek from Massalia who sailed into the North Atlantic, had this new spirit. Perhaps the most outstand-ing symbol of the Hellenistic Age was, fittingly, a city founded by Alex-ander himself—Alexandria, on the Mediterranean Sea at the western edge of the Nile Delta. With the breakup of Alexander's empire, one of his Macedonian generals, Ptolemy, made this port city the capital of his new kingdom based in Egypt.

THE PTOLEMIES SUPPORT EXPLORATION

Ptolemy had accompanied Alexander all the way to the Indus River and back. He took up Alexander's idea of an expedition to Arabia and spon-sored an expedition under an admiral, Philo. Philo sailed down along the African side of the Arabian Sea, but did not discover any new lands. Following his return, however, the Egyptians under Ptolemy began to import elephants and ivory from Africa south of Egypt. Ptolemy I's son and successor, Ptolemy II Philadelphus, established trading ports along the Red Sea and opened up trade with Yemen and Somalia. He also sent explorers to the coast of the Horn of Africa. Other members of the Ptolemaic dynasty, as this family of rulers of Egypt are known, sent still more expeditions to this region.

Although these expeditions were mostly concerned with trade, each journey increased the store of knowledge of these little-known places. One of the most ambitious explorers of this era was Eudoxus. He came from Cyszicus, a city in northwest Turkey. Eudoxus's first expedition took place under Ptolemy VIII Euergetes II, who ruled the kingdom from 146 to 111 B.C. As the story went, "an Indian happened

(opposite page) Pictured is Alexander the Great's empire at its height. He conquered the Persian Empire and much of the world as it was known to the Greeks at that time.

to be brought to the king by the guards of the Arabian [Gulf], who said they found him cast ashore alone and half dead, but who he was and whence he came they did not know because they could not understand his language." After the Indian was taught Greek, "he promised to be a guide on a voyage to India for men chosen by the king." Eudoxus is among those who went. When he returned loaded with precious stones and other valuable objects, however, Euergetes took all (or most of) his cargo. When Euergetes died, his widow sponsored another expedition to India. Again, Eudoxus returned with valuable goods and again the new king seized his cargo.

THE LIGHTHOUSE AND LIBRARY OF ALEXANDRIA

Under Ptolemy I and his successors, Alexandria became one of the most important cities of the ancient world. It was a center of both trade and culture. Alexandria is famous today for two great structures: the lighthouse and the library. The lighthouse, one of the Seven Wonders of the Ancient World, was designed by Sostratos, a Greek. It stood some 440 feet (134 m) high on a small island in the city's harbor. A continually burning fire provided the light that could be seen far at sea by the many ships approaching the city with their goods—and tales—from all over the world. Built about 270 B.C., it collapsed during an earthquake about A.D. 730.

The library, established by Ptomely I but greatly expanded by his son, contained copies of virtually every existing written work known. These were in the form of scrolls, most of them made of papyrus, the early form of paper. Some were parchment, made of animal skin. The library is believed to have had about 700,000 scrolls.

The great library of Alexandria was more than a place to deposit written works. It also was a center of scholarly and scientific studies. Its chief librarians, its staff, and its visiting scholars made this the world's premier center of knowledge about the world for several centuries. The library was eventually destroyed during several attacks on the city.

One would think that Eudoxus would quit at that, but while returning on that second voyage, he had been blown ashore on the east coast of Africa. Not knowing how large Africa was, he now decided to sail around it and head straight for India, thus avoiding the Ptolemies. His plan was to head first for Africa's west (Atlantic) coast. He fitted out a ship and sailed across the Mediterranean, along the way taking on all kinds of cargo expected to trade in Africa and India. He sailed through the Pillars of Hercules and then rounded the northwest shoulder of Africa. Before long his ship ran aground and was wrecked. After building a new ship, he sailed a bit farther. He soon turned back, intending to make a new voyage in a larger ship. In fact, Eudoxus probably had gone only slightly south of Morocco.

After several adventures in northwest Africa, he made his way to Spain. There, he built two more ships and organized yet another expedition to reach India. Even Strabo remarks: "How was it that [Eudoxus] did not fear . . . to sail again." He sailed off once more into the Atlantic and down the west coast of Africa—and was never heard of again. Some scholars question just how much of Eudoxus's story is true. Others accept it and regard Eudoxus as having earned a place in the history of exploration.

THE LEGACY OF OTHER GREEKS

The Ptolemaic dynasty ruled Egypt. The rest of Alexander's vast empire was divided up among several of his former generals and their heirs. One of these was Seleucus I Nicator, who by 312 B.C. assumed control of the territory that included Mesopotamia and Persia. Although a tough military man, Seleucus was also interested in knowing more about the world he lived in. Why? To exploit it, of course. About 285 B.C., he sent a man named Patrocles on an expedition to the Caspian Sea. Patrocles sailed along the southern edge of the sea, noting the various rivers that entered there. He returned with claims that the Caspian Sea opened into a northern ocean. He also claimed that it was connected by a water route to India. These claims would mislead the Greeks for some time to come.

Meanwhile, an Indian by the name of Chandragupta Maurya had seized power in northeastern India. By about 305 B.C., he had forced Seleucus to give him control over the region once occupied by

Alexander's forces. Chandragupta built a new capital at Pataliputra on the Ganges River. Seleucus wanted to maintain good relations with his neighbor. So, in 302 B.C., he sent an ambassador there. He chose Megasthenes, a Greek of considerable learning. Megasthenes wrote the *Indica*, a complete account of India—its geography, climate, government, people, customs, and religion.

Large parts of the *Indica* were preserved in the texts of other ancient authors, including Strabo and Arrian. *Indica* was for many centuries the most respected work on India in the West, and modern scholars, by comparing his statements with those of Indian accounts of that time, have confirmed that Megasthenes was far more accurate than most of his contemporaries. Megasthenes knew, for instance, that the Indus River flowed from northeast to southwest. He knew that the Ganges River also started in that direction but then turned eastward and that the Himalaya Mountain range ran across the northern boundary of India. He also knew that the summer monsoon season caused great floods.

Another Greek of the Hellenistic era who wrote about his own observations of Earth was Posidonius. Posidonius was born in Syria about 135 B.C. He wrote on a variety of subjects. It is his works on meteorology and the ocean that contributed most to the ancients' knowledge of Earth. Drawing on his extensive travels throughout the Mediterranean region and into France (and possibly as far as Britain), he wrote about the depth of that sea, the role of earthquakes and volcanoes in forming particular features of the landscape, and, most important, the influence of the Sun as well as the Moon on producing the highest "spring" tides. So influential was Posidonius that, unfortunately, his wrong calculation of the circumference of Earth was long accepted instead of the correct calculation by Eratosthenes, a Greek mathematician and astronomer of the third century B.C.

By the time Posidonius was writing, the Hellenistic world was changing. Most of the former lands of Alexander were no longer ruled by the descendants of those Macedonians and Greeks who divided up Alexander's empire. Instead, a new power was in control. That power was Rome, and it was about to control an empire even larger than Alexander's.

6

The Romans

As late as 600 b.c., the Romans were a group of people living on farms. Over the next 325 years, they gradually extended their power over much of the Italian peninsula. They had accomplished this by military might, to be sure, but they had also succeeded by establishing colonies of Romans throughout Italy. They did this by building roads, by forming political alliances, and by a general tolerance of the cultures of the peoples whom they conquered. In time their empire extended from the North Atlantic to the Caspian Sea and Persian Gulf.

As successful as they were as empire builders, the Romans were not great explorers in the conventional sense. Their military forces certainly moved into remote lands; their traders visited lands far from Rome; and they wrote books about familiar and exotic places. Yet, for all their boldness in extending the borders of their empire, they never really ventured into the unknown. In the roll call of great explorers, there are virtually no Romans. During the many centuries that the Romans were so dominant, however, they contributed greatly to consolidating what was known about the world.

THE ROMANS EXPAND

Having taken over Italy south of the Alps by 275 b.c., the Romans set their sights on the rest of the Mediterranean world. First, they confronted the major power in the western Mediterranean, the port city of Carthage. This colony belonged to the Phoenicians. In the Punic Wars (246 b.c. to 146 b.c.), the Romans drove the Carthaginians out of their colonies in the western Mediterranean—Sicily, Sardinia, Corsica, and Spain. In 146 B.C., they captured and destroyed Carthage itself. Rome was now master of the western Mediterranean and a large part of North Africa.

To its north and northeast, Rome faced many challenges. Tribes from France invaded northern Italy, but were defeated in 225 B.C. During the next one hundred years, Rome took control over the peoples

The Phoenician port-city of Carthage (present-day Tunisia) was a rich and major power in the Mediterranean. Its rivalry with Syracuse and Rome led to a series of wars with respective invasions of each other's homelands. The Romans captured Carthage in 146 B.C., and then completely destroyed the city to prevent the Carthaginians from ever challenging them.

along the northern frontiers of the Alps and all the way from Portugal and Spain across southern France to the Dalmatian coast, the western shore of the Adriatic Sea.

Meanwhile, Romans took over what was left of Alexander's Hellenistic empire in the east. By 189 B.C., Rome had defeated Antiochus III, grandson of Seleucus I who had ruled the empire in Asia, and took control of the coastal lands and islands of the eastern Mediterranean. In 196 B.C., Rome had defeated the Macedonians under Philip V. It gained Alexander's original kingdom that included Greece and Macedonia. In 146 B.C.—the same year that Rome destroyed Carthage—Rome crushed all resistance in Greece by destroying its great city of Corinth.

During the next 100 years, Rome continued to expand. Numidia, a kingdom in northwest Africa (roughly today's Algiers), was reduced to a Roman province after 46 B.C. At the other end of their empire, in 63 B.C., Rome gained Alexander's old empire in Syria and Asia Minor.

The Romans had put their empire together in about 200 years. They had done so in the face of almost constant resistance by the conquered peoples and internal struggles among various Roman leaders. There is little to suggest, however, that they had much interest in these new and distant lands except to exploit their resources. Perhaps the one major exception, Polybius (ca. 203 B.C.–120 B.C.), himself a Greek under the patronage of a powerful Roman general, traveled throughout parts of Spain, Gaul (France), the Alpine region, and northwestern Africa. In the book *Universal History*, Polybius focused mostly on historical events, and was constantly describing the geographic features of the settings of these events. He said "what men want to know is, not so much the fact that a thing took place as the way in which it happened." His assertion that traveling to places was important to any historian or geographer— "for the eyes are more accurate witnesses than the ears"—was, in effect, an endorsement of exploration.

The first Roman who put this into practice was a man who, for all his many achievements, never thought of himself as an explorer: Julius Caesar.

JULIUS CAESAR THE LEADER

Julius Caesar was born into a wealthy Roman family in 100 B.C. Like many young men of his class, he went off to Athens to study philosophy and oratory (speech-making). He next put in some time with the Roman army. When he returned to Rome, it was with a burning desire to achieve public office. In 65 B.C., he was placed in charge of Rome's department of the public works and state-sponsored games. He used this office to gain favor with the masses, much to the annoyance of more conservative Romans. By 62 B.C., Caesar became Spain's praetor—a cross between a supreme justice and a military governor. In 59 B.C., he was elected one of the two consuls, the most powerful job in Rome. A man could only serve as consul in Rome for one year. After that year, he was assigned the right to rule over one of Rome's provinces, including the right to command an army there. Caesar was assigned to Cisalpine Gaul—Gaul "this side of the Alps," meaning northern Italy—and Transalpine Gaul (Gaul beyond the Alps). Today, the countries of this land include France, parts of Belgium, Germany, and Switzerland.

In 58 B.C., Caesar moved into Gaul. He planned to put down the many rebellions of its people. Caesar would later write of this land: *Gallia omnis divisa in partes tres*. "All Gaul is divided into three parts." For the next nine years, Caesar led an almost constant series of campaigns and battles, putting down the Gauls west of the Rhine River in France, and at one point crossing the Rhine—the first Roman general to do so. He did this while chasing rebellious Germanic tribes. He wanted them to know the power of Rome.

In 55 B.C., he did something even more daring. He led a small force across the Strait of Dover to the island of Britain. In this trip, he barely moved beyond the coast, but in 54 B.C. he took a larger force. This time he moved inland, crossing the Thames River some 80 miles (128 km) from the coast. Caesar met little opposition.

After a few months, Caesar returned to Gaul to pursue Rome's enemies there. After achieving his greatest victory—the defeat of the Gallic chieftain, Vercingetorix, in 52 B.C.—he anticipated that he would be welcomed back to Rome as the conquering hero. His rivals, however, did not trust him and he was told to give up command of his army on January 1, 49 B.C. Instead, Caesar led 5,000 of his most loyal men to the border between his provinces and Roman Italy.

From this point on, Caesar's story becomes one of the great dramas of history. His rapid conquest of Italy, his appointment as dictator, his pursuit and conquest of his Roman enemies from Spain to Egypt, his

In 49 B.C., Julius Caesar led his army across the Rubicon River in northeastern Italy, thus committing himself to an act of treason against the authorities in Rome. This episode is depicted above by an early nineteenth-century artist. "Crossing the Rubicon" is now a popular phrase meaning to pass a point of no return.

affair with Egyptian queen Cleopatra, his numerous reforms and populist measures, his attempts to conciliate the conservatives—all swept aside by the strokes of the swords of the men who assassinated him on March 15, 44 B.C.

JULIUS CAESAR AND THE HISTORY OF EXPLORATION

Julius Caesar deserves a place in the history of exploration because of one book he wrote: *De Bello Gallica*, or "Commentaries on the Gallic War." Caesar's own account of the campaigns from 58 through 52 B.C. is regarded as one of the masterworks of classical literature. Written in a crystal-clear style, Caesar not only describes his strategies, tactics, and battles but also writes of the natural features and peoples of Gaul. Greek and Roman traders and merchants had been visiting Gaul for centuries. Most Greeks and Romans knew more about the lands and peoples to their east, however. Caesar brought western Europe into the circle of the known.

Above all, Caesar described many basic geographic features of the vast territory. He often identified quite accurately mountains, rivers, coastlines, and plains. Of course, he was not always correct in his details. Thus he describes the island of Britain:

> *A triangular island with one side, about 500 miles [804 km] long, opposite Gaul; one end of this side, the one in Kent, faces east, the other faces south. The second side, 700 miles long [1,126 km], faces Spain and the west; on this side is Hibernia [Ireland], half as large as Britain, and between them is Mona [Isle of Man]; there are thought to be several other islands where, according to some writers, at the time of the winter solstice, night lasts for thirty days. The third side of Britain, 800 miles [1,287 km] long, faces north and there is no land opposite; one end of this side is toward Germany.*

Caesar was wrong both about the total length of Britain's "sides." He was also wrong about the orientation of the island in relation to continental Europe. Nonetheless, Caesar's reputation caused more Romans than ever to become interested in Britain. In time Romans would return to conquer much of the island.

AUGUSTUS AND THE PAX ROMANA

Rome was not formally declared an empire until Julius Caesar's adopted son and chosen successor, Gaius Julius Caesar Octavianus, became emperor in 27 B.C. At that time he took the name Augustus. Augustus continued to expand the boundaries of the Roman Empire, although largely at its fringes—in North Africa, northern Spain, and Asia Minor. One major addition was a large strip in Europe that extended Rome's dominion up to the Danube River and included most of what is today Switzerland, southern Germany, Austria, Hungary, the former Yugoslavia, and Bulgaria. The other was Egypt, which was reduced to a Roman

ALL ROADS LEAD . . .

An old saying states that "all roads lead to Rome." Rome was not the first ancient state to build roads—the Persian Empire was famed for its roads—but most of the pre-Roman roads outside cities were not paved. It was the Romans who built the most extensive system of intercity paved roads. The first great Roman road was the Via Appia, begun in 312 B.C., to lead from Rome to Capua (just north of Naples). By 244 B.C., it went to Brindisi on the eastern coast opposite Greece. In 220 B.C., the Romans built the Via Flaminia to lead northeastward to the Adriatic coast; starting in 187 B.C., it was extended northwest to Placentia (modern Piacenza), creating a stretch that became known as the Via Aemilia; eventually it was extended to Genoa as the Via Julia Augusta III. About 130 B.C., Rome built the Via Egnatia, which stretched all the way from the modern Albanian port of Durres on the Adriatic coast, across Macedonia and northern Greece, to the great city of Byzantium (later Istanbul). Those were the great roads, but there were many more throughout the empire. These roads were not just paved on the surface—with either flagstones, gravel, or concrete—they were solidly constructed, often with foundation layers that were four feet (1.2 meters) deep. High-ranking officials were made responsible for their upkeep, and they did their job so well that many stretches of the Roman highway system remained in use 1,500 years later. Some even can be traveled on today.

province in 31 B.C. after the defeat of Egypt's queen Cleopatra and her Roman husband, Marc Antony, at the battle of Actium, off the west coast of Greece.

During his long rule from 44 B.C. to A.D. 14, Augustus did something even more important than enlarge the empire. He created peace and order across the land by maintaining a disciplined army even at the most remote frontier outposts. In addition, Augustus assigned responsible administrative officials, set up a postal system, built more roads. The Romans even took exact measurements of the distances between towns.

It was the policies of Augustus that began the famous *Pax Romana*—the Roman peace that endured for some 225 years throughout the empire. Roman soldiers and sailors, merchants and traders, craftsmen and entrepreneurs, spread out through the empire, introducing Roman ways to other peoples and introducing other peoples' ways to Romans. The Pax Romana also created the conditions that encouraged people from all over the vast empire to venture forth. Times were peaceful, so people traveled.

After Augustus died in A.D. 14, he was followed by a series of rulers who left the empire much as it had been. One major exception, however, was Rome's gradual conquest of Britain. This campaign began under Claudius, who ruled from A.D. 41–54. It took Rome 400 years to completely control Britain.

One way to look at Rome's empire was that it simply put Alexander's empire back together, added some more lands, and then advanced even further the sophisticated spirit from the Hellenistic Age. Peoples from all over the Roman Empire regarded themselves as citizens of a new world. Although there are no major discoveries or great individual explorers during this period, there were numerous writings that advanced people's knowledge of this great empire.

The two great historians/geographers of this era were Strabo (63 B.C.–A.D. 21), a Greek by descent, and Pliny the Elder (A.D. 23 –A.D. 79). Strabo traveled simply to inform himself while Pliny traveled primarily on military or governmental assignments. It is to their writings that future generations owe a great deal. Strabo's *Geography* was a major survey of the world, all the way from India in the east to the Scilly Islands off Britain's southwesternmost coast, and from northern Europe to Ethiopia in Africa. He is the sole source of many of the earlier accounts of explorations.

Pliny the Elder combined a career in the military with that of a writer. Of his many volumes only one work survives, the *Naturalis Historia*. It drew from hundreds of other authors to present an encyclopedia

(opposite page) Under the leadership of Augustus Caesar, adopted son and chosen successor of Julius Caesar, Rome achieved great glory. During his reign, Augustus expanded the boundaries of the Roman Empire from central Italy to the entire Mediterranean world.

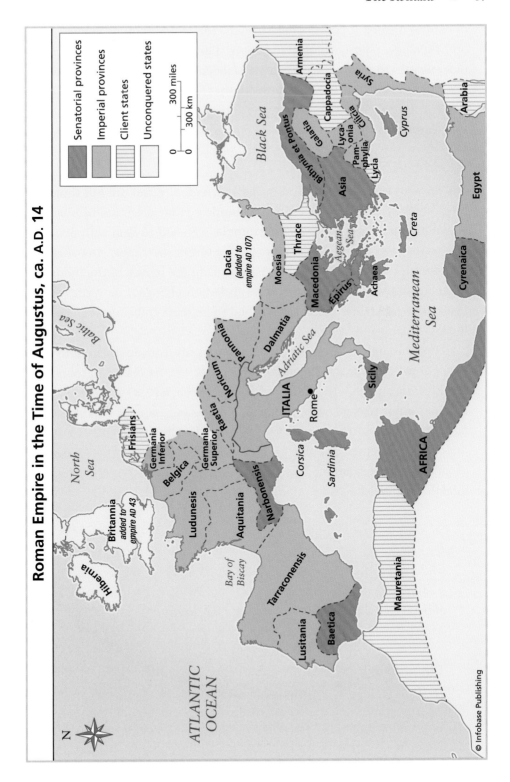

Roman Empire in the Time of Augustus, ca. A.D. 14

Legend:
- Senatorial provinces
- Imperial provinces
- Client states
- Unconquered states

0 — 300 miles
0 — 300 km

ATLANTIC OCEAN

Hibernia

North Sea

Baltic Sea

Britannia *added to empire AD 43*

Frisians

Germania Inferior

Belgica

Ludunesis

Germania Superior

Raetia

Noricum

Pannonia

Dacia *(added to empire AD 107)*

Black Sea

Armenia

Bithynia et Pontus

Galatia

Cappadocia

Cilicia

Lyca-onia

Pam-phylia

Asia

Lycia

Syria

Cyprus

Arabia

Egypt

Aquitania

Narbonensis

ITALIA

Rome

Corsica

Sardinia

Dalmatia

Adriatic Sea

Moesia

Thrace

Macedonia

Epirus

Achaea

Aegean Sea

Creta

Cyrenaica

Sicily

Mediterranean Sea

AFRICA

Mauretania

Baetica

Lusitania

Tarraconensis

Bay of Biscay

N

© Infobase Publishing

of natural history. It described geography, zoology, botany, mineralogy, anthropology, pharmacology, and more. Pliny included writing from older writers that would have otherwise been totally lost. Although he was not a scientist, it was his curiosity that led to his death. When he saw that the volcano Vesuvius was erupting in August 79, he sailed to the nearby coast to get a closer look. He was killed by poisonous gases.

ROME AND THE EAST

The Romans took great interest in their own empire, but did not show much interest in the world beyond its borders. They preferred to leave exploration to others. Greeks, for example, were left to deal with peoples to the east. In the first century A.D., a Greek merchant, Hippalus, sailed from the tip of the Arabian Peninsula to the mouth of the Indus River. In the winter, when the wind direction changed, he returned from India to Arabia. His voyage helped to increase trade between the Roman Empire and India.

Hippalus and his achievement are known only from another anonymous Greek's work, the *Periplus Maris Erythraei*, or "Sailing around the Erythraean Sea." The book, written between A.D. 50 and 90, was a sailor's guide to the coasts of Africa, Arabia, and India. It details the natural features of the coasts, the cities, and each city's exports and imports. It was clearly a guide for merchants, but it also included basic geographical information. This passage describes the extremely strong tidal flow of the Mahi River along the west central coast of India:

> *So great indeed is the violence with which the sea comes in at the new moon, especially during the nightly flow of the tide, that, while at the commencement of its advance, when the sea is calm, a sound like the shouting of an army far away reaches the ears of those who dwell about the estuary, and shortly afterwards the sea itself with a rushing noise comes sweeping over the shallows.*

This periplus is important for another reason. Although the author seems to have firsthand knowledge only down to about 500 miles (804 km) northwest of the tip of the Indian peninsula, he mentions places much farther away. He reports a distant land where "there is a great inland city called Thina, from which raw silk and silk yarn and silk cloth are brought overland." Although scholars cannot agree on what city he was referring to, they tend to agree that the people producing the silk were probably Chinese. This is one of the earliest references to the Chinese in Western accounts.

Silk itself was by no means an unknown product in the West at this time. In the first century B.C., Roman historians reported that silk was used to make awnings for Julius Caesar's ceremonies and for Cleopatra's dresses. Clearly, though, it was a luxury reserved for the most powerful. Even the Romans who knew about silk remained uncertain about its source as they obtained it through middlemen at the fringes of their empire. It would not be long, though, before Rome would deal directly with China and Asia. Europeans would discover a continent with its own long history in the field of exploration.

7

China's and Asia's Role in Exploration

WHILE AUGUSTUS RULED, ROME APPEARED TO BE THE HUB OF Earth. Not only did all roads—and sea routes—lead there, the produce of the world was transported there. This included the basics such as grains and olive oil, as well as luxury items like incense, ivory, precious stones, and silk. Meanwhile, the armies and administrators of Rome were stationed from the Atlantic to the Nile. Thus, it has seemed reasonable to trace the story of discovery and exploration as radiating out from there.

The fact is, peoples in other parts of the world had long been exploring and discovering. Many of these peoples did not have writing systems, so there is little or no record of the many individuals who ventured forth into distant parts. One people in particular, however, can boast of a history as well documented and as distinguished as any in the West. They are the Chinese.

CHINA'S EARLY PHASE

Human beings appeared in China as early as any place in the world—about 50,000 B.C.—but China's traditional history begins around 2800 B.C. It was not until the Shang dynasty (ca. 1750–1040 B.C.) that a written language appeared. Historians consider China's written accounts to be a fairly accurate version of events.

From 1750 to 221 B.C., China was a land in almost constant turmoil. It was by no means a unified nation and certainly not one that embraced all the territory of modern China. Yet China had its own tradition of geographical writings. The oldest of these texts that has survived is the *Shu Ching,* meaning "the Classic of History." It dates to about 450 B.C., the same time of the great Greek historian/geographer Herodotus. The *Shu Ching* describes the land and resources of China and sounds much like a textbook:

> *Between the Chi river and the Yellow River is the province of Yen (the second province). The nine branches of the Yellow River were led into their proper channels. The Lei-hsia district was made into a marsh, and the Yung and Chu rivers joined it. The mulberry grounds were stocked with silkworms, and the people descended from the hills and dwelt in the plains. The soil of this province is black and fat, its grass is luxuriant and its trees are tall.*

These early Chinese took a scientific interest in describing their world. In its systematic detailing of geographic features, in fact the *Shu Ching* was more advanced than any comparable text in the West.

Another book from this era is the *Shan Hai Ching* (Classic of the Mountains and Rivers). Its contents appear to date from several periods, extending from at least 300 B.C. to A.D. 200. It also contains geographical information. However, this is combined with legend and myth and fantasy. There are tales of winged men, dog-faced men, bodies with no heads, and heads that fly about alone. There are similar tales in Herodotus's writing, but whereas Herodotus's travels can be traced along known routes, the journey described in the *Shan Hai Ching* is regarded by scholars as purely imaginary:

> *[I] have walked about three hundred li [1 li = approx. 1/3 of a mile] since Bald Mountain. Here, Bamboo Mountain is near the river that looks like a boundary. There is no grass or trees but some jasper and jade stones. . . . three hundred li to the south, Bald Mountain is found . . . wild animals are found here that look like suckling pigs, but they have pearls. . . . Three hundred li farther south, Bamboo Mountain is found, bordering on a river. . . . There is no grass or trees but there are many green-jasper and green-jade stones.*

THE HISTORIC PERIOD

The Qin (Ch'in) dynasty (221 to 206 B.C.) was the first to impose a certain unity over China. It built roads and waterways to improve communication. It was the Qin dynasty that also commenced building the Great Wall along China's northern border to hold back marauding tribes.

The Qin dynasty was soon replaced by the Han dynasty (202 B.C.– A.D. 220). The Han is generally recognized as providing the foundations of modern China. By the time Wudi assumed the throne in 141 B.C., the Han had established a strong central government. During his 54-year reign, he expanded the dynasty's power in all directions—including into Korea. In particular, Wudi wanted to know more about the Yuezhi peoples far to the west. He wanted to make an alliance with them against China's enemies, the Xiongnu, who lived to the northwest of Han China (today's Mongolia). In 139 B.C., Wudi hired Zhang Qian, a court official, to explore the lands west of China.

Zhang Qian proceeded west but was soon captured by the Xiongnu. They held him captive for 10 years—he even married one of their women and had a son with her—but eventually he was able to escape. He continued west to a region today belonging to Uzbekistan and Kyrgysztan. He was unable to persuade the people there to join the Han against the Xiongnu, so after about a year with them he headed back. Once again, Zhang Qian was captured by the Xiongnu. This time he escaped after only about a year.

Emperor Wudi rewarded Zhang Qian with the post of a palace counselor. Although he had failed to enlist allies against the Xiongnu, he brought back a great deal of information about this region, including an account of a larger breed of horses than the Chinese had available. He also brought back samples of grapes, walnuts, and pomegranates. If Zhang Qian wrote an account of his adventure, it did not survive.

(opposite page) Archaeological findings have provided evidence of advanced, multilevel societies in ancient China dating back to the Shang dynasty (c. 1750–1040 B.C.). The Yellow River basin, also called "the cradle of Chinese civilization," was the most prosperous region in early Chinese history. In January 2009, on the banks of the Yellow River, Chinese archaeologists uncovered the largest horse and chariot pit so far found in China, dating from the Shang and Zhou dynasties.

Everything that is known about him comes from one of the most famous works of Chinese history, *Records of the Grand Historia*, by Sima Qian (ca. 145 to 90 B.C.):

> *Anxi [Persia] is located several thousand li west of the region of the Yuezhi's land. The people live on the land, cultivating the fields and growing rice and wheat. They also make wine out of grapes. They have walled cities. . . . the region contains several hundred cities of various sizes. . . . Tiaozhi {Mesopotamia] is situated several thousand li west of Anxi and borders the Western Sea [Persian Gulf]. It is hot and damp, and the people live by cultivating the fields and planting rice. . . . When I was in Daxia [Bactria, now northern Afghanistan], I saw bamboo canes from Qiong [a Chinese region] and cloth made in the province of Shu [another Chinese region]. When I asked people how they had gotten such articles, they replied, "Our merchants go to buy them in the markets of Shendu [India]." Shendu, they tell me, lies several thousand li southwest of Daxia.*

Zhang Qian's description of these lands and their people interested Wudi. About 125 B.C. he asked Zhang Qian to lead a second expedition to Daxia. This expedition was divided into four groups to find the best way through hostile peoples. None of the groups managed to get as far as Zhang Qian had reached on his first journey. Some did manage, however, to bring back a number of the larger horses. These were quickly adopted by the Han cavalry.

THE SILK ROAD

Something even more important came out of Zhang Qian's journeys and report. The Chinese began to send caravans carrying goods overland to the west, avoiding the indirect sea route through Southeast Asia and then the middlemen in India. Their route came to be known as the "silk road." It passed from eastern China into central Asia, and from there across the Middle East to the Mediterranean. There was not one single road, but at least two major roads across China—one a northern route, one the southern route—and several branches off these two routes. All roads tended to meet at Kashgar, today known as Kashi (or

K'oh-shih), in the farthest west of China and still a major commercial center for all central Asia. The caravans were made up of horses, mules, camels, and wagons. The Chinese and other Asians who led them only went as far as Kashgar. There, traders from other nations took over the goods. At least one more middleman usually carried the goods before reaching the Mediterranean Sea and western Europe.

Caravans coming from China to the west carried silk, spices, furs, ceramics, jade, bronze objects, iron objects, exotic plants, and animals. Meanwhile, caravans heading east from the West carried ivory, gold, precious stones, and glass. Along the road, goods were exchanged—often more than once—so not all the goods that finally reached one end of the route had started out at the other end.

In time, there were more and more contacts between the Chinese and Westerners. About A.D. 435, Fan Ye had a "Chapter on the Western Regions" that discussed China's relations with the Arab world of about A.D. 25–55. It described the people of northern Saudi Arabia and Jordan. Between A.D. 92–102, Ban Chao, the protector-general of the Silk Road, went almost to the Caspian Sea and returned with information about the Romans. Gan Ying, a Chinese envoy traveled all the way to Antioch, Syria, about A.D. 97. He wrote an account of the people living there, at that time a province of Rome. Gan Ying wrote that "the people there are honest in their transactions and do not double their prices."

By about A.D. 160, there were many links between the Mediterranean and Asia. India especially provided an alternative route from the Silk Road and served as an intermediary for trade goods. They could count on caravans making their way overland between the Mediterranean and China. Sailors and traders who lived along the Persian Gulf, Arabian Sea, and Indian Ocean brought these goods up to the shores of Egypt or Arabia. (Roman coins from this period have been found at places all along this route and even as far east as Cambodia.) Likewise, the Chinese could count on obtaining wares from Africa, India, and the Middle East from middlemen in central or Southeast Asia. Mariners and merchants moved all along the coasts of India, Malaysia, the Indochina peninsula, and the East Indies islands exchanging the goods of China and Europe. Despite all this traffic, there were no known explorers making their way between Europe and Asia during this period.

Zhang Qian's colorful stories to local rulers about central Asia made people desire goods from other areas. An East-West trade route soon developed and was named the Silk Road. Caravans, like the one depicted, traveled the great superhighway of its age. It was used not only for trading goods but also for relaying information and ideas between the East and the West.

ON THE TRAIL OF BUDDHISM

One thing that was making its way to China from India was the Buddhist religion. By about A.D. 65, a half brother of Emperor Mingdi of China adopted Buddhism, and Buddhists were tolerated in the capital. One story tells that Mingdi saw the Buddha in a dream, and then sent men to India to learn about his teachings. The men returned about the year 67 with Buddhist books and statues. They even brought two Buddhist monks who started translating the Buddhist writings into Chinese. This story may be only a legend but by the year 166, Buddhism was recognized at the royal court. In 170, Lokakshema, a Buddhist monk, arrived in China. He began to translate some of the Buddhist texts into Chinese. Within 25 years, large Buddhist communities were flourishing in eastern China.

With the end of the Han dynasty in A.D. 220, China entered into a long period of unrest. Along the Silk Road, trading traffic declined because the Chinese were not able to maintain order. In China itself, Buddhism spread among the masses. It offered consolation during a time of earthly sufferings. Many Chinese Buddhists made pilgrimages to India, much as Christians would later travel to Jerusalem or Muslims to Mecca.

In the year 399, Faxien, a 65-year-old Chinese Buddhist, set off for India to obtain some of the sacred Buddhist texts. He walked across central China and the Taklamakan Desert in far western China, then crossed Tajikistan and entered India. He reached Tamluk (near modern-day Calcutta), a stronghold of Buddhism. The trip had taken several years, and he spent several more in India before boarding a ship for home. He spent three more years on his trip. Faxien arrived home in northern China in 413.

Faxien carried back with him Buddhist texts and images. More importantly, he carried his notes and memories of his travels. These he set down in 414 as the *Record of Buddhist Countries* (more widely known today as *Travels of Faxien*). Faxien wrote about the history and customs of the peoples he passed through in Central Asia and India, especially of the role of Buddhism in their lives. Thus he says of Yu-teen in far western China:

Yu-teen is a pleasant and prosperous kingdom, with a numerous and flourishing population. . . . They all receive their food from the common store. Throughout the country the houses of the people stand apart like stars, and each family has a small stupa [a small Buddhist shrine] erected in front of its door. . . . In the monasteries they provide rooms for monks traveling from all quarters and who are provided with whatever else they require.

BUDDHISM ACROSS ASIA

Siddhartha Gautama founded Buddhism in India about 500 B.C. He came to be known as Buddha, "the Enlightened One." Buddhists believe in a cycle of death and rebirth for all people. The only way to escape from this is to give up earthly things. Doing so will help a person reach nirvana, or perfect peace and happiness.

Buddhism also asks its followers to respect all forms of life, to free their minds from evil, to control their feelings and thoughts, and to practice concentration of mind and body. What might seem curious at first glance is that the Buddhist religion, which appears to call for a rather passive approach to the world, spread so rapidly all the way to China. Yet the true believers in Buddhism, mostly monks who devoted their entire existence to their beliefs, were active in promoting their faith by their presence and their writings. In ancient times, these monks helped Buddhism spread quickly from India into neighboring lands such as Nepal, Indonesia, Burma, and Sri Lanka. Buddhism also spread to the peoples living along the Silk Road. From there it began to attract the Chinese people.

Buddhism did not always find it easy going in China. China had its own faiths, Confucianism and Taoism. These faiths would help shape a Chinese form of Buddhism. In the course of moving into China, Buddhism also drew many Chinese to explore the world beyond their own land's boundaries. By the mid-sixth century, Buddhism had spread to Japan.

Faxien was one of the most adventurous travelers of his time. By his example and his writings, he helped to inspire even more Chinese to travel to India. This increased traffic between India and China opened up lands between and around these two vast countries.

By Faxien's time—the fifth century A.D.— the Chinese had written and collected an impressive number of geography books, some of them dealing with foreign lands on their borders. They also showed a great interest in mapmaking. At the same time, there was still a tradition of storytelling. One of the more curious stories from China's history is said to have been recorded in the *Liang-shu* (Records of the Liang dynasty), an account of the dynasty that ruled southern China from A.D. 502–557. Hwui Shan, a Buddhist priest, arrived at the court of the Liang king in 499. He claimed that he had just come from Fu-sang, which lay far to the east of China—that is, way off across the Pacific Ocean. His account of this place went on as follows:

> *It produces many fu-sang trees from which it derives its name. . . .*
> *Its fruit resembles the pear, but is red; the bark is spun into*
> *cloth for dresses and woven into brocade. The houses are made*
> *of planks. There are no walled cities with gates. The people use*
> *characters for writing, making paper from the bark of the fu-*
> *sang. There are no soldiers wearing metal armor for they do not*
> *carry on war.*

Hwui Shan went on to describe Fu-sang's criminal justice system, the ruler's clothing, social classes, and wedding and burial customs. Along with Hwui Shan's account, there were other Chinese tales of places that seemed to be part of or nearby Fu-sang. One was called the "Kingdom of Women," where there was a "black canyon," a "smoking mountain," a "sea of varnish," and a "sea the color of milk." Here, too, the people lived in round houses, some men had dog heads, and some women married snakes. Most scholars consider these things along with the whole story of Fu-sang as sheer fiction, but that has not stopped many people from insisting this proves that the Chinese got to the Americas by about A.D. 500.

By the fifth century A.D., the Chinese had written a number of geography books that told of foreign lands. Elaborate tales about a far-off place called Fu-sang, which had plants similar to present-day Mexico's maguey, or agave plant *(pictured above)*, lead some people to believe that the Chinese had reached America by about A.D. 500.

They locate Fu-sang and the Kingdom of Women in places from British Columbia to Mexico and find analogies in Native American cultures. Thus the fu-sang tree is said to be anything from the prickly pear to the agave plant, known in Mexico as the maguey. The "black canyon" is today said to be the Black Canyon of the Gunnison National Monument in west-central Colorado; the "smoking mountain" is the still-active Volcán de Colima in Mexico; the "sea of varnish" is the La Brea Tar Pits near Los Angeles; the sea "the color of milk" could be one of several dried-up salt-bed lakes in California; the round houses are the adobe houses of the Navajo or Pueblo Indians of the American Southwest; the men with dog heads referred to the masks worn by the Hopi in their Kachina ceremonies; and the women who married snakes referred to a Hopi legend of the origin of their Snake Clan.

Interestingly, it is mostly Westerners, not Chinese, who have chosen to promote this theory. The Chinese came to call their country *Chung-kuo,* which means "Middle Kingdom." They thought of China as the geographical center of the world and the true center of civilization. For all their careful work in the fields of geography and mapmaking, they saw little need to go forth and explore the world. Instead, they withdrew behind their borders and expected the world to come to them.

8

A World Closes In

By the second century A.D., great changes had taken place in the world since the first civilizations began in both the Middle East and Asia some 3,000 years earlier. New lands had been discovered. These lands were explored and settled. Kingdoms and dynasties and empires had come and gone. Now the world was divided into several main power centers. The Roman Empire ruled from western Europe to the Middle East. China ruled its homeland well across into central Asia and down into parts of Southeast Asia. India was powerful in South Asia. Due to the work of sailors, traders, and missionaries these regions were aware of one another's existence, even if much of the information was false. However, there were still large gaps in people's knowledge of what made up Earth.

PTOLEMY'S WORLD

One of the major centers of the world in the second century A.D., out-ranked only by Rome, was Alexandria, Egypt. This was the city founded by Alexander the Great. Although Rome now ruled Egypt, Alexandria continued to be a highly cosmopolitan city. Its library probably exceeded anything in Rome as a center of intellectual activity. Basically the library was a university research center for all branches of the sciences, literary studies, and historical texts. One of its most famous scholars in the middle of the second century was Claudius Ptolomaeus, known today as Ptolemy. Ptolemy was famed for his work in astronomy, mathematics, optics, and geography.

Almost nothing is known about this man. His name hints that he was Greek. He wrote his works in Greek. He may have been related to the Ptolemies who had ruled Egypt for almost 300 years until the last of the dynasty, Cleopatra, died in 30 B.C. Ptolemy must have been born about the year A.D. 100 for he is known to have started his astronomical observations about the year A.D. 127. He published a series of groundbreaking works in the sciences, but almost all the books were lost. They are known only because Arabic scholars translated them. These were eventually translated into Latin and later into other European languages.

The work that had the greatest influence on the Western world was Ptolemy's *Geography* and its maps. The book shows how Ptolemy viewed Earth, and his maps brought together all that people outside Asia knew of Earth. He used lines on his maps showing latitudes and longitudes much like those in use today. He even knew enough to curve them to account for the spherical shape of Earth. Unfortunately, these lines become increasingly less accurate as he moved farther and farther beyond the Mediterranean area.

Ptolemy's understanding of the world was surprisingly accurate in some instances. He seemed to have quite detailed knowledge of the coastline of Britain (although he had Scotland turned on its side). He recognized that the Caspian Sea was landlocked, not joined to the ocean as so many before him believed. He knew about the Carpathian Mountains in eastern Europe, the Volga River in Russia, and the sources of the Nile River in two African lakes. He described the overland trade route from the Euphrates River to northern China.

At the same time, Ptolemy made mistakes. He did assume that there was some unknown *Terra Australis,* or "southern land." However, he had it connecting the southern end of Africa to the southern corner of China. Much of Germany, eastern Europe, and Russia were left blank. He thought Scandinavia was an island and drew Sri Lanka 14 times larger than it is. Most seriously of all, he misjudged the total circumference of Earth. He made it almost 30 percent smaller than it is. Needless to say, he had no place on his maps reserved for the Americas.

Yet despite all these errors, Ptolemy's writings on geography and his maps were the most accurate to come out of the ancient world. Such was his reputation that they would remain the standard for centuries. This is not to say that most people on Earth were even aware of Ptolemy's work. His writings vanished into obscure libraries, and his maps disappeared altogether. It was not until the 1400s, in fact, that European scholars began to reconstruct his maps by using his very detailed books. By that time, scholarship in Europe had fallen into such a low state that Ptolemy was regarded as an absolute authority. His maps and books would influence almost all the early explorers, including Columbus, and contribute to their miscalculations about the distances to be traveled and the location of lands.

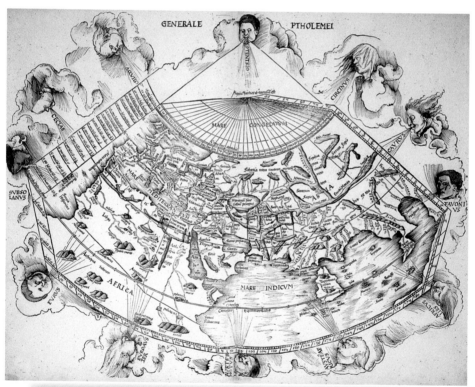

Above is a fifteenth-century copy of Ptolemy's world map, taken from one of his most famous texts, *Geographia*. It shows the countries of Serica and Sinae (China) at the extreme east beyond the islands of Taprobane (Sri Lanka) and Aurea Chersonesus (Malaysia). Much of Ptolemy's data is inaccurate. Still, Ptolemy's work would influence almost all of the early explorers.

THE ORIGINAL TOURIST: PAUSANIAS

Many Romans were widely traveled and wrote down huge amounts of information about the known world. But it was a Greek from one of the empire's distant provinces who first showed the curiosity of today's travelers. His name was Pausanias. He was a Greek who probably came from Asia Minor (a region now part of modern Turkey) and prospered around A.D. 150. Judging from various remarks in his only known book, he may have been a doctor. He was also interested in bird watching. It is clear that he traveled at least through Palestine, Egypt, and parts of Italy. Above all, he visited all the major sites in central and southern Greece. Then he wrote his observations in about A.D. 155 in his *Itinerary of Greece*.

Pausanias's book was written in Greek. It was filled with detailed descriptions and historical background about all the important classical sites. It also had practical information about road conditions and hints about how to save time or see lesser-known curiosities. Pausanias's book stands out from other books of its time in that it is based not on others' work but on his actual visits to every one of the places he describes. To this day, people can still visit these sites in Greece and use Pausanias's work as a guidebook.

THE DECLINE OF EXPLORATION

Ptolemy stood out because during the next 1,200 years few others were doing much mapping of Earth, at least in the West. From the third century, China was developing its own quite scientific system of map-making. But the Chinese shared the same limitation of Ptolemy's work. Their "scientific" maps were based on their astronomical observations and mathematical calculations, not on firsthand knowledge of the world nor on the reports of sailors or travelers. In other words, they were not based on the information of explorers.

This was not necessarily the fault of the mapmakers. There were very few libraries and no newspapers or magazines in which to report current findings. For that matter, only a small number of people could read and write. There was a fundamental "disconnect" in all societies in that era. There was simply a lack of scientific knowledge, technology, and inventions. People lacked the means to know exactly where rivers and mountains and lakes were located. They could not calculate precisely the distances between places on land as well as sea.

Rome, for example, certainly counted many highly intelligent people within its far-flung boundaries. Few of them, however, seemed to have been interested in breaking new ground. Instead, they were more devoted to what might be called "secondhand scholarship." Some of the writers on geography and exploration during the early centuries of Roman power who have already been quoted often provide the sole accounts of early explorers.

But there does seem to have been another level to this "disconnect." Even people in a position to do so did not seem to be motivated to send forth or go forth to seek out new lands. Even if they did, and if they did write up reports, no records survived them. There were a few exceptions, among them the several surviving periploi (plural of periplus), meaning "circumnavigations." A few of the earlier ones have been drawn on already. These include the account of Hanno's voyage down the northwestern coast of Africa and the account of Pytheas's voyage to Britain and the North Atlantic.

There were several more of these in the later part of the Roman Empire. In A.D. 131, Arrian, the Roman historian, wrote a *Periplus of the Euxine Sea*. This was a guide to the coast of the Black Sea. *The Stadiasmus of the Great Sea*, dated to sometime in the third or fourth centuries, was a guide to a large section of the coast of the Mediterranean Sea. It not only gave fairly exact distances but provided information about harbors and depths of water along the way. Another such work of this era, dated about A.D. 400, was written by Marcianus of the Greek city Heraclea. It described the "Outer Seas," which referred to the Indian and Atlantic oceans.

There were also books that described an overland route. *The Parthian Stations* of Isadore of Charax (probably somewhere in Persia) recorded the route from Mesopotamia to India during the reign of Augustus. The *Itinerarium Antonini*, written about A.D. 200, records the main routes and towns throughout the Roman Empire at that time. The *Jerusalem*

Itinerary, dated to the fourth century A.D., provides detailed instructions for Christian pilgrims to make their way from France across Italy to Constantinople and then down as far as Antioch, then a center of Christianity in Syria.

SHUTTING DOWN

As interesting and informative as these many books were, they were all guides to known places. They all "wrapped up" the world rather than left it open-ended. What is notable, too, is that almost none of the historians or authors of guides were themselves Romans. The Chinese of this time were the opposite. They wrote about and charted only Chinese expeditions. Yet, they were like the Romans in that they were not interested in journeying into the unknown. In fact, for all their careful work in the fields of geography and mapmaking, the Chinese—with few exceptions—did not show much interest in exploring the world far beyond their borders. Perhaps the symbol of this was the Great Wall. True, it was designed to hold off potentially hostile neighbors, but by A.D. 500 it had come to symbolize China's determination to remain isolated.

It was almost as though the world needed to take a break about the year 500. By this time, people lived on almost all the world's major landmasses. The exception, of course, was Antarctica. People would not live there until the twentieth century. The world's population around the year A.D. 500 has been estimated to have been about 300 million to 500 million. This was not that many by today's standards. Many large areas of land were still uninhabited.

Many isolated islands far off in the oceans were still unknown. The most outstanding instance was New Zealand. It would probably not be until sometime between A.D. 750 and 1000 that the first humans came ashore there. They were the Maoris from Polynesian islands to the north of New Zealand. Some ancestors of the modern Inuit had made their way to Greenland centuries before A.D. 500, but there is some question as to whether they stayed there. In any case, it was still unknown to Europeans. European sailors knew about Iceland but it was still uninhabited by anyone. Madagascar was perhaps the last of the world's largest islands to remain unsettled, but by the year 500, people had been coming there from Indonesia and Africa.

Virtually every corner of Africa, Asia, and Europe was known to and settled by at least some people. Although it was unknown to the rest of the world, the entire Western Hemisphere, from the Arctic region to the tip of South America, was at least sparsely inhabited.

By the year 500, much of the world did seem to be in disarray, if not in complete turmoil. The Roman Empire had split into Western and Eastern empires in 395. For decades the Western empire was repeatedly attacked. By 476, the last Western emperor was defeated by a Germanic leader, Odoacer. War between the tribes of Europe and the Eastern empire soon followed.

China, too, was divided into northern and southern kingdoms. Each kingdom was under attack from both internal and foreign forces. India was likewise being torn apart. Its enemies were both invaders from central Asia and competing Indian kingdoms. It was not a good time to set out for new lands. New generations and new peoples would have to take up the search.

Ancient peoples were handing over an impressive legacy. Their view of the world was greatly flawed. It was full of gaps, misconceptions, and errors. Even the best-informed people still did not know the true locations and dimensions of most of Earth's territories. Ancient peoples' motives for moving into new territories, moreover, were often less than noble and their methods were often brutal. Yet people today should hesitate before finding fault with these ancients. Just consider what they endured to travel to distant points! Sea voyages were uncomfortable and dangerous. Journeys overland were unbelievably difficult. The ancient world definitely deserves recognition for contributing its share to the history of discoveries and explorations.

WHAT CHARACTERIZES ANCIENT EXPLORERS?

Many ancient peoples deserve great credit for their contributions to the discovery and exploration of new lands. However, many others did not engage in this activity. Just why did some people show no interest in seeking out new lands?

Even several of the ancient peoples encountered in this book have shown little interest in exploring new lands. The Egyptians, for example, were largely content to stay close to the Nile. The Romans, for all the vast territory they dominated, did not seem to take much initiative in seeking out the unknown. The Chinese did send out expeditions, but then they stopped this and drew within their circle.

Meanwhile, there are ancient peoples who seem to have shown no interest in moving outside their own culture's base. The Maya of Central America began to emerge as early as 1500 B.C. They reached the height of their civilization between about A.D. 200–800. During this long period of time they made astronomical observations that allowed them to work out extremely precise calendars. They developed a sophisticated number system that included something like a zero. They developed a system of writing more advanced than any used by other Native Americans. They built technically sound architecture and ambitious ceremonial centers. They constructed stone-surfaced roads and irrigation

At its peak (A.D. 200-800), the Maya of Central America had one of the most fully developed societies in the world. The Maya developed large-scale, independent city-states in well-known cities like Copán (in present-day Honduras). Pictured is part of a ball court that was found at a Mayan site in Copán. The game involved knocking a small rubber ball through a vertical hoop. It appears that the losers were decapitated as sacrifices.

systems. They traded a variety of products over great distances with their fellow Maya, often using large canoes that moved along the coast.

Yet for all these accomplishments, the Maya do not seem to have ever ventured very far from their own homeland, a confined region extending from Mexico's Yucatan Peninsula in the west to the highlands of Guatemala in the east. Even their wars were fought among themselves. They seemed to show no interest in expansion or exploration. They are one of the prime examples of a self-contained society.

The Huns were a totally different type of society. They were a nomadic people based in the steppes of Mongolia. Some scholars believe that they were the people known to the Chinese as the Xiongnu. The Xiongnu began to invade northern China as early as the second century B.C. Led by Attila between 433 and 450, Huns moved westward into Europe. Eventually Attila ruled an empire extending from the Caspian Sea in the east to the Rhine River in the west. Not satisfied with this, Attila invaded Gaul (modern France) and northern Italy. Local peoples, Roman troops, famine, and disease stopped the Huns. Attila was killed in a battle north of present-day Venice in 453. The Huns retreated to Asia.

The Huns, then, were the complete opposite of the Maya. They were almost always on the move over a vast territory. However, they established no major cities and developed no important culture. They left no material remains. Instead of being self-contained, they exist almost entirely as a people who intruded on other peoples. Yet, like the Maya, they seem to have shown no interest in exploring new lands. The Huns were interested only in taking over the lands of others.

The Maya and the Huns do not represent the only types of ancient societies. There were other groups who showed no interest in discovering and exploring new lands. Why is this so? Just what distinguishes explorer cultures from non-explorer cultures? Are there some underlying and unifying factors? These are all questions that might lead to stimulating discussions.

There is probably no single factor that makes a society engage in exploration. But one thing is clear: The ancient people described in this book's chapters do seem to have shared at least one characteristic. They all have the ability to consider the unknown, to recognize that something must lie beyond familiar borders.

Chronology

c. 6300 B.C.	Oldest known dugout (boat) linked to Holland.
c. 4000 B.C.	The Sumerians develop first small, powerful city-states in Mesopotamia (encompassing modern Iraq, parts of northeastern Syria, parts of southeastern Turkey, parts of southwestern Iran).
c. 3200 B.C.	Unified Egyptian kingdom is founded by King Menes, giving rise to a series of dynasties that lasts for the next 3,000 years.
c. 2350 B.C.	Sargon of Akkad conquers Sumerian city-states. He soon controls southern Mesopotamia, the region to his east (modern Iran) and west (Syria, Palestine, and Turkey). Regarded as the first ruler to create a multiethnic, centrally ruled empire.
c. 2000 B.C.	First people to eventually become known as Greeks emerge. Starting in 1500 B.C., they begin to migrate throughout the Mediterranean to trade with other peoples.
c. 1492 B.C.	Queen Hatshepsut sends Egyptian ships down the Red Sea and into the Indian Ocean to the Land of Punt (Somaliland or India), establishing trade between the two lands.
c. 1200 B.C.	Phoenicians are already dominant mariners in the eastern Mediterranean. They start founding colonies in the western Mediterranean.
c. 800 B.C.	Major Phoenician trading center, Carthage (on the coast of North Africa), is founded.
c. 600 B.C.	Major Greek trading center, Massilia, is founded.
c. 550 B.C.	First Persian Empire, the Achaemenid Empire, is formed. Reaches its peak during reigns of Darius the Great (521–486 B.C.) and Xerxes the Great (486–465 B.C.).
c. 509 B.C.	Traditional date for the founding of the Roman republic.

c. 500 B.C.   Carthaginian explorer Himilco is first to reach northwestern shores of Europe.

c. 492–449 B.C.   Persian Wars (490 B.C. Battle of Marathon; 480 B.C. Thermopylae; 479 B.C. Salamis and Plataea).

c. 483 B.C.   Buddha dies.

c. 479 B.C.   Confucius dies.

c. 450 B.C.   Greek historian Herodotus ("the Father of History") travels widely throughout Greece, Mesopotamia, the Phoenician coast, Egypt, the eastern coast of North Africa, and all the way to southwest Russia. Writes about his travels and the people he met along the way in *The Histories*.

Timeline

c. 4000 B.C.
The Sumerians develop first small, powerful city-states in Mesopotamia

c. 2000 B.C.
First people to eventually become known as Greeks emerge

c. 800 B.C.
Major Phoenician trading center, Carthage (on the coast of North Africa), is founded

c. 509 B.C.
Traditional date for the founding of the Roman republic

c. 4000 B.C.   c. 500 B.C.

c. 3200 B.C.
Unified Egyptian kingdom is founded by King Menes, giving rise to a series of dynasties that lasts for the next 3,000 years

c. 1200 B.C.
Phoenicians, already dominant mariners in the eastern Mediterranean, start founding colonies in the western Mediterranean

c. 500 B.C.
Carthaginian explorer Himilco is first to reach northwestern shores of Europe

- *Shu Ching*, the oldest surviving geographical text from China, is written. It is a survey of the land and resources of China.

c. 334-325 B.C. Alexander the Great conquers much of what was then the civilized world. He was the first great conqueror to reach Greece, Egypt, Asia Minor, and up to western India.

c. 315 B.C. Greek geographer and explorer Pytheas of Massilia makes voyage of exploration of north-western Europe. Pytheas travels around much of Great Britain, is the first on record to describe the Midnight Sun, first to mention the name

c. 264–146 B.C.
Rome conquers Carthage, becoming the most powerful state of the western Mediterranean

c. 315 B.C.
Pytheas of Massilia makes voyage of exploration of northwestern Europe

c. A.D. 500
All of the world's landmasses are inhabited, except for Antarctica

c. 450 B.C.

c. A.D. 500

c. 450 B.C.
Greek historian Herodotus writes about his extensive travels in *The Histories*; at about the same time *Shu Ching*, the oldest surviving Chinese text is written

114 B.C.
Zhang Qian expands the central Asian part of an extensive interconnected network of trade routes called the Silk Road

27 B.C.–A.D. 180
Rome has peace for 200 years, called Pax Romana

	Britannia and Germanic tribes, and the first to state that the moon influences the tides.
300 B.C.–A.D. 100	Buddhism spreads throughout Asia.
c. 264–146 B.C.	The largest wars of the ancient world, the Punic Wars, are fought between Rome and Carthage. Hundreds of thousands of deaths on both sides; Rome conquers Carthage, becoming the most powerful state of the western Mediterranean.
c. 221 B.C.	Construction begins on the Great Wall of China during the Qin dynasty and continues for about 1,700 years. The wall was built along 1,200 miles (1,931 km) of China's northern border to hold back marauding tribes. The Qin dynasty also builds highways and waterways to enable better communication.
139 B.C.	Zhang Qian is hired by China's Emperor Wudi to explore the farthest western reaches of China and central Asia.
114 B.C.	Zhang Qian expands the central Asian part of an extensive interconnected network of trade routes called the Silk Road. Trade on the Silk Road was a major factor in the development of the civilizations of China, India, Egypt, Persia, Arabia, and Rome.
44 B.C.–A.D. 14	Augustus reigns over Rome and expands the empire and secures its boundaries with client states. Much of the city is rebuilt and public government projects are instituted. His rule initiates an era of relative peace that lasts for more than 200 years, called the Pax Romana (27 B.C. to A.D. 180).
c. A.D. 175	Astronomer/geographer/mathematician/astrologer Ptolemy publishes a series of works, three of which continue to be important to Islamic and European science. Ptolemy's *Geography* is surprisingly accurate in some cases.
c. A.D. 500	All of the world's landmasses are inhabited, except for Antarctica (which would not be settled until the twentieth century).

Glossary

astrolabe—An instrument invented as early as 200 B.C. to measure the level of elevation, or altitude, of the sun, stars, or planets. Originally used by astronomers (*astrolabe* in Greek means "star taker"), it would eventually be adapted for use in navigation.

cauldron—A large vessel usually used for boiling liquids.

circumnavigate—The term is from the Latin for "sailing around," and refers to sailing around a large body of land, whether an island, a continent, or the entire earth.

cuneiform—The system of writing employing small wedge-shaped (Latin *cuneus* means "wedge") elements pressed into wet clay tablets by a stylus (see **stylus**). It was invented by the ancient Sumerians about 2500 B.C. and adopted by many of the peoples who lived across Mesopotamia and Persia during the next 2,500 years.

dead reckoning—A method long used by navigators to estimate the position of a ship at sea based on such factors as the time in passage from a known point, the (estimated) speed of the ship, and changes of direction in relation to (noninstrument-aided) observations of celestial bodies. The term *dead* is thought to come from the word *deduce,* meaning to trace from a beginning.

Druid—A member of an order of priests in the religion practiced in ancient Gaul and Britain. The word has come to be applied to anyone who practices that religion.

dynasty—A succession of rulers from the same family or line that maintains a certain continuity of practices.

estuary—The point at which a river's mouth meets the sea and so the ocean's tides affect the river's current.

fossil—The remains—usually only a part but they could be complete—of a plant or animal that had lived in the distant past. (*Skeleton* is usually used to refer to bones less than many thousands of years old.) The term may also refer to traces of living organisms, such as footprints or outlines of a plant. Often it refers to bones of humans or other animals that have been embedded and preserved in earth or rock.

gnomon—A device that casts a shadow from the sun and is used as an indicator of time or location; a sundial is the most familiar example.

head—When used in connection with a body of water, it refers to the top, or closed end, of a gulf or bay.

hominid—A member of the family that includes the direct ancestors of human beings as well as all living human beings. It is generally recognized that the hominid line began about 5 million years ago.

Homo erectus—Latin for "upright man," this term refers to the stage in human evolution extending from about 1,800,000 to 750,000 years ago, the time when the ancestors of modern humans first began to walk in an erect position.

Homo sapiens—Latin for "knowledgeable" or "wise" man, this term refers to the species of human being that first appeared about 160,000 years ago and to which all modern humans belong.

homogeneous—All of the same or similar kind.

insurrection—An open revolt or uprising against a civil authority or established government; often it is begun by a small and relatively unorganized group, and it may at least start with civil disobedience rather than warfare.

interstices—In the context of mining, it refers to narrow spaces in rocks where the desired mineral is located.

Inuit—The major group of Arctic people living across northern Canada and Greenland. This name is now preferred instead of Eskimo, which among other problems fails to distinguish among various other Arctic peoples such as the Aleut and Yup'ik.

jade—One of two minerals—jadeite or nephrite—that are usually pale green or white stones. When polished, jade is used either as gemstones or for carvings.

kybernetes—A Greek word for "governor" or "controller," it was the ancient Greeks' term for a ship's helmsman. In the 20th century, it was adopted for *cybernetics,* the study of control processes in biological, mechanical, and electronic systems, and from this the word *cyber* was spun off to be applied to many things related to computers.

lacquerware—Objects whose surface has been treated with lacquer, originally a natural resin from the lacquer tree found only in Asia. In modern times, a lacquer finish may be applied with synthetic compounds. Lacquerware has a hard, shiny surface.

latitude—The angular distance north or south of the earth's equator and measured in degrees. Sometimes referred to as a *parallel,* there are 90 degrees between the equator and each of the poles.

li—A standard ancient Chinese unit of measurement of distances; although there is some disagreement as to its exact equivalent, most scholars consider it to equal about 1/3 a mile.

longitude—The angular distance east or west of the modern prime meridian, Greenwich, England. It is measured in degrees; there are 360 degrees altogether, measured as up to 180 degrees east or west of Greenwich.

middleman—In commercial transactions, an individual who buys from producers or other traders and then sells to other traders, merchants, or consumers.

monsoon—A major wind system that reverses directions seasonally and thereby affects large climatic areas. In southern Asia in particular, it is a wind from the south or southwest that brings heavy rains in the summer, and the first mariners from Europe had to learn about the monsoon in order to plan their voyages in the region.

nomadic—Describing a group of people who have no permanent home but move—usually according to the seasons—in search of food and water for themselves or grazing lands for their animals.

pathogen—Any biological agent that causes disease; it usually refers to living microorganisms such as bacteria or fungi or to viruses.

periplus—(plural *periploi*) From the Greek word for "sailing around," this term is used for the published directions for mariners for coastal routes and points of interest along these routes.

pilgrimage—A trip undertaken to a sacred place or religious shrine.

praetor—A Roman official, originally a supervisor of the administration of justice. Over time, the position changed, becoming more like a military magistrate in the provinces. Under the empire, the praetors returned to being administrators of the law, but their power declined and the title became little more than honorary.

quern—A stone, usually with a recessed surface, on which grain or other crops are ground by a handheld tool.

rationalist—An individual who believes in relying on reason as the best guide to understanding and activity. In ancient Greek history, this was applied to the school of intellectuals who first appeared in Ionia, the Greek-based region along the coast of Turkey, and it characterized many Greek philosophers' approach to life.

stylus—The instrument used to write cuneiform, its sharp end is wedge-shaped—that is, slightly wider at one tip than the opposite.

truss—A rigid framework designed to support a structure; in the case of shipbuilding, it would be a horizontal beam extending between the two sides of a hull to maintain the ship's shape.

wattle—A structure made of poles intertwined with branches, twigs, or reeds; the term may also refer simply to the materials used to make such a structure.

Bibliography

Aubet, Maria Eugenia. *The Phoenicians and the West: Politics, Colonies and Trade.* Cambridge, UK: Cambridge University Press, 2001.

Barton, Miles. *Prehistoric America: A Journey through the Ice Age and Beyond.* New Haven, Conn.: Yale University Press, 2003.

Bosworth, A. B. *Conquest and Empire: The Reign of Alexander the Great.* Cambridge, UK: Cambridge University Press, 1993.

Bunson, Matthew. *Encyclopedia of the Roman Empire.* Rev. ed. New York: Facts On File, 2002.

Cavalli-Sforza, Luigi Luca. *The Great Human Diaspora: The History of Diversity and Evolution.* Trans. by Sarah Thorne. Cambridge, Mass.: Perseus Publishing, 1996.

Cunliffe, Barry. *The Extraordinary Voyage of Pytheas the Greek.* Rev. ed. New York: Walker & Co., 2003.

Dillehay, Thomas. *The Settlement of the Americas.* New York: Basic Books, 2000.

Fagan, Brian. *People of the Earth: An Introduction to World Prehistory.* (With CD) Upper Saddle River, N.J.: Prentice Hall, 2000.

Fraington, Karen, ed. *Historical Atlas of Expeditions.* New York: Facts On File, 2001.

Fox, Robin Lane. *Alexander the Great.* New York: Penguin Group (USA), 1994.

Gaines, Ann Graham. *Herodotus and the Explorers of the Classical Age.* New York: Chelsea House, 1993.

Herodotus. *The Histories.* Trans. by Aubrey de Selincourt. New York: Penguin Group (USA), 2003.

Higham, Charles F. W. *Encyclopedia of Ancient Asian Civilizations.* New York: Facts On File, 2004.

Lambert, David, ed. *Encyclopedia of Prehistory.* New York: Facts On File, 2002.

Lauber, Patricia. *Who Came First? New Clues to Prehistoric America.* Washington, D.C.: National Geographic, 2003.

Markoe, Glenn. *Phoenicians.* Berkeley: University of California Press, 2001.

Morkot, Robert, ed. *The Penguin Atlas of Ancient Greece.* New York: Penguin Group (USA), 1997.

Obregon, Maurice. *Beyond the Edge of the Sea: Sailing with Jason and the Argonauts, Ulysses, the Vikings and Other Explorers of the Ancient World.* New York: Modern Library, 2002.

Roseman, Christina Horst. *Pytheas of Massalia: On the Ocean: Text, Translation and Commentary.* Chicago: Ares Publishing, 1994.

Scarre, Chris, ed. *Penguin Historical Atlas of Ancient Rome.* New York: Penguin Group (USA), 1995.

Sorenson, John L., and Martin Raish. *Pre-Columbian Contact with the Americas Across the Ocean: An Annotated Bibliography.* 2nd ed. rev. Provo, Utah: Research Press, 1996.

Stockwell, Foster, and Sharon L. Lechter. *Westerners in China: A History of Exploration and Trade, Ancient Times Through the Present.* Jefferson, N.C.: McFarland & Co., 2002.

Wachsmann, Shelley. *Seagoing Ships and Seamanship in the Bronze Age Levant.* College Station: Texas A&M University Press, 1998.

Further Resources

FICTION

Bell, Albert A., Jr. *All Roads Lead to Murder.* Stratford, Victoria, Australia: Publishing, Ltd., 2002.

Cole, Les. *The Sea Kings.* Ventura, Calif.: House of Adda Press, 1996.

Ford, Michael Curtis. *The Ten Thousand.* New York: St. Martin's Press, 2002.

Leckie, Ross. *Carthage.* Edinburgh, Scotland: Canongate Books, 2001.

Manfredi, Valerio. *Alexander—The Ends of the Earth.* New York: Washington Square Press, 2002.

Renault, Mary. *Fire from Heaven.* New York: Vintage Books, 2002.

——. *Funeral Games.* New York: Vintage Books, 2002.

——. *The Persian Boy.* New York: Vintage Books, 1998.

Scarrow, Simon. *Under the Eagle: A Tale of Military Adventures and Reckless Heroes with the Roman Legions.* New York: St. Martin's Press, 2001.

Turteltaub, H. N. *Over the Wine Dark Sea.* New York: Tor Books, 2002.

Vidal, Gore. *Creation.* New York: Doubleday, 2002.

Waltari, Mika. *The Egyptian.* Chicago: Chicago Review Press, 2003.

DVD

Egypt: Rediscovering a Lost World (2005). BBC Warner, DVD, 2005.

Egypt's Golden Empire (2002). PBS Paramount, DVD, 2005.

The Greeks: Crucible of Civilization (1999). PBS Paramount, DVD, 2005.

Rome: Power and Glory (1998). Questar Inc., DVD, 2000.

Silk Road (1991). Central Park Media, DVD 3-Disc Set, 2002.

WEB SITES

**Encyclopedia Phoeniciana—A Bequest Unearthed, Phoenicia
http://phoenicia.org**
The world's largest Web compilation of resources and studies about the origin, geography, religion, culture, etc, of the Canaanite Phoenicians.

**History Link 101, Ancient Cultures
http://historylink101.com/index.htm**
Online source for information about the cultures of Africa, Aztec, China, Egypt, Greece, Mayan, Mesopotamia, Rome, Olmec, Prehistory, Middle Ages, and

World War II subjects. Contains 2,000 images, along with maps, biographies, and other types of resources.

Illustrated History of the Roman Empire
http://roman-empire.net
The leading Web resource on Rome. Information includes articles, video, maps, photographs, links to other sites, a current events calendar, and a section just for young readers.

Travel China Guide: Silk Road
http://www.travelchinaguide.com/silk-road/
Site dedicated to those interested in traveling to China, including various tours of the Silk Road. Includes historical information, photographs, and planning suggestions.

Picture Credits

Index

About the Contributors

Author and general editor **JOHN S. BOWMAN** received a B.A. in English literature from Harvard University and matriculated at Trinity College, Cambridge University, as Harvard's Fiske Scholar and at the University of Munich. Bowman has worked as an editor and as a freelance writer for more than 40 years. He has edited numerous works of history, as well as served as general editor of Chelsea House's AMERICA AT WAR set. Bowman is the author of more than 10 books.

General editor **MAURICE ISSERMAN** holds a B.A. in history from Reed College and an M.A. and Ph.D. in history from the University of Rochester. He is a professor of history at Hamilton College, specializing in twentieth-century U.S. history and the history of exploration. Isserman was a Fulbright distinguished lecturer at Moscow State University. He is the author of 12 books.